MOTHER

BY

E. F. BENSON

Copyright © 2013 Read Books Ltd.
This book is copyright and may not be
reproduced or copied in any way without
the express permission of the publisher in writing

British Library Cataloguing-in-Publication Data
A catalogue record for this book is available from the
British Library

E. F. BENSON

Edward Frederic Benson was born at Wellington College (where his father was headmaster) in Berkshire, England in 1867. He was educated at Marlborough College, where he proved himself as an excellent athlete, representing England at figure skating, and published his first novel, *Dodo* (1893), when he was 26. The novel was quite popular, and Benson eventually expanded it into a trilogy (*Dodo the Second*, in 1914, and *Dodo Wonders*, in 1921). Nowadays, Benson is principally known for his 'Mapp and Lucia' series about Emmeline "Lucia" Lucas and Elizabeth Mapp. The series consists of six novels and two short stories, and remains popular to this day, being serialized for Radio 4 as recently as 2008. Benson was also a respected writer of ghost stories – indeed, H. P. Lovecraft spoke very highly of him, especially his story 'The Man Who Went Too Far'. Benson died of throat cancer in 1940, aged 72.

Photo: *H. Walter Barnett & Co., Ltd.*]

MARY BENSON.
(Aged 75.)

[*Frontispiece.*

PREFACE

FOR many years my mother regularly kept a diary in which she recorded matters of public and domestic interest, the comings and goings of her family and friends, appreciation of people and of books, and often very caustic criticism of both. But she kept also a more intermittent and far more private chronicle, contained in half a dozen casual notebooks of various shapes and sizes, the earliest of which deals with her childhood, and was written some years later. She was married at the age of eighteen, and with her married life the account becomes contemporary with what it records. There are gaps in it, some of which extend over many years, and it deals entirely with intimate and personal affairs. She tabulates certain rules of life which she set up for herself with regard to her devotions, her exercise, and so forth, but it is chiefly concerned with the problems, the darknesses and illuminations, which came to her soul.

I brought these little books down here one spring, and, reading and re-reading them, learned more than I had ever known about her joys and sadnesses, her fears and her courage. Much therein was too private ever to be published; of the rest I have made considerable use. Should any reader think that I have exceeded the limits of due discretion, my excuse must be that I believed it could only benefit him to learn something of the inner history of a life so beautiful as hers.

She, then, is the central figure of the following pages, which comprise the years from my father's death in 1896 to her death in 1918.

E. F. B.

LAMB HOUSE,
    RYE.

CHAPTER I

AT the moment when, as he knelt in the church at Hawarden, my father's spirit went forth without struggle or any pang of parting, the ship of my mother's purposes and activities in life slipped its moorings. It slid away from the busy quay-side and, as if grounding on some remote and barren shore, left her to disembark on an emptiness, a nothingness. All those who loved her and were loved by her with all the force and fire of her humanity were for the time but phantoms in the mist; nobody else but he was real to her. She carried with her nothing except the lantern of her trust in God, but that she kept trimmed and burning. Even if it only showed her an impenetrable darkness, no ray of it was quenched.

In spite of her eager devotion to her children and her intimacy with her friends, in spite, too, of her vivid interest in life as such, no one in those days, except him, had any real existence for her, and it could hardly have been otherwise. She was now fifty-five years old, and since her marriage at the age of eighteen, she had dedicated herself and all the activities of her life to him. That dedication, in fact, had been made seven years before her marriage, for when my father first knew her (she being of the mature age of eleven) he had absolutely made up his mind that she was to be his wife, and had written her a poem which clearly told her so.

The sketch of those seven years before her marriage, as recorded by her in certain reminiscences, which, sharp as a newly etched plate, she put down some twenty years later, reads like some extraordinary and imaginary romance of a child. But it was the actual story of her life which she there recorded, the faithful prelude to the forty years which followed. My father, who was her second cousin, was at that time a master at Rugby, and lived with her mother and her and her three brothers, William, Henry, and Arthur Sidgwick. There was he, twenty-three years old, masterful and convincing and convinced, writing his first love-poem to his cousin of eleven, sure in his own soul that Minnie was to be his wife as soon as ever she was old enough, and carrying that conviction through both to her mother and her. My grandmother heard of the love-poem from one or both of them, and very properly put a veto on his carrying his courting any further at present, but that seemed to have been a very ineffectual bar to his ardency, for my mother records how, though he had been forbidden to speak to her on any such subject, till she was old enough to realize what he was talking about, there was soon another interview when he held her hand and kissed her, and embarked again on the forbidden topic. It is quite clear that he was entirely to blame for breaking this very proper prohibition, but, ever so characteristically, she blames herself for it, not him, and tells how she felt that she had been guilty of disloyalty to her mother who had forbidden what we must call such " goings-on."

It is delightful to linger over this picture of herself, these compromising confessions and her criticisms on her own character. She allows rather grudgingly that she was of a sunny and merry nature, but deplores the truth of her mother's account of her to a friend, when she said that " Minnie is more volatile than the other children." She loved pleasure and hated pain, but found the pain of others more unbearable yet; " I always longed to take it away and make them happy *at once*." All these seven years of my father's waiting for her were full of " resolves " dictated by the supreme longing to be worthy of him. One " great resolve," it seems, came to her as she returned home after her confirmation, and she made the elastic band round her prayer-book the witness thereof, so that whenever her prayer-book was in her hand, she would be face to face with her resolve. That was very like her: the unrecorded " resolve," to the end of her life was never sufficient; it had to go down in her diary, signed and dated, with the penalty of confession often attached to the breaking of it. . . .

Glimpse by glimpse in this intimate mirror of herself there becomes manifest a background of shadowy misgiving. She became aware that though (accepting her coming marriage as something augustly and inevitably preordained) her main desire in life was to please Edward and not disappoint him, she surrendered herself to his influence rather than to the instinct of her own love: she had not chosen him as he had chosen her. " I was happiest," she says, " when I knew Edward to be happy, and yet wasn't with him," and she records her dread of displeasing him at her lessons with him in architecture, physical geography, and German; she did not feel towards him the love that casts out fear. All her energies were bent on the desire " to be worthy of him, to please him, not to disappoint him," dedicating all that she knew of her own nature to his service and his love. Her mirth, her charm, her eager desire " to make people happy at once " were his.

On the other side was my father, a volcano of physical and mental energy, twelve years her senior, choosing her with ardent affection, and at the same time seeing in the gaiety and sweetness of her someone to educate. He longed for her to be put into his hands that were as strong as they were loving, to mould her into a noble womanhood. He had no such notion of self-surrender as she had, and though he had never probably put it to himself that it was he to whom she was to conform, he certainly saw himself as the instrument which, in God's hands, should fashion her. He never imagined himself fused in her ; he saw her fused in him, and his passion for her, furiously sincere, had not in it that incense of worship, out of which is begotten the supreme tenderness, whereas in her nature that tenderness was the chief emotional ingredient. He intended that his love should sweep her into his view which regarded life as an arduous splendid battlefield in the wars of God, that by her marriage with him she should consecrate herself not to him only nor to him mainly, but to the species of service which his nature demanded of him, without realizing that thus she would have to cease being herself altogether and to become someone entirely different. But he could no more have changed that instinct of hers to make things pleasant for other people and take away their pain, where a sterner moralist would have let them remain uncomfortable if by that means the sufferer might be induced to learn some bracing lesson, than she could have made him dilatory in duty or indulgent to a fault. That was not his way : he pounced on a fault (quite rightly) with a view to its correction ; she (quite rightly), without condoning the sin, would set to work to comfort the sinner.

So, when she was just eighteen, they were married, and she tells how she instantly saw not her mistake (for if her marriage was a mistake, what marriage since the world began was a success ?), but the quality of his love, and, with nothing but pity for him, her own poverty. " An utter child," she writes, " I danced and sang into matrimony with a loving but exacting, a believing and therefore expectant spirit, twelve years older, much stronger, much more passionate, whom I didn't really love. But let me try to realize how hard it was for Edward. He restrained his passionate nature for seven years and then got me, this unloving, weak, unstable child. I know how disappointing this must be to him, how evidently disappointed he was. How hard for him, full of all religious and emotional thoughts and yearnings. They had never awoke in me. . . ."

Directly after her marriage, her contemporary diaries, reminiscences no longer, begin. This dominant desire to please him, not to fail him, not to disappoint him, was the standard she at once set herself to live by in the early days of her marriage ; his approval was the measure of her success. She mentions, for instance, a small dinner party at which " in the drawing-room afterwards, feeling it was rather dull, I actually was bold enough to sing ! Miss Wickenden helped me, and we got through ' Willie, we have missed you ' ; ' Wait for the waggon ' ; and ' Long time ago.' . . . I don't know whether it was wise of me or not, but certainly I did not vex Edward, and I think that is as good a criterion as I need have. . . ." Next day she records how " Edward has talked to me so lovingly and gently lately. He said not long ago with such an earnest eager look and his eyes full of tears, ' Minnie, if you will only try, I will never be cross with you again.' I, instead of answering him as he deserved, said, 'Are you sure?' 'Yes, sure,' he replied, 'but you must remember that your promise will be as hard to keep as mine.' I can never doubt his love. Oh, to think of really being a true wife to him! God help me! I believe I shall persevere this time. If I can only stir up my apathy I can do a great deal."

She records occasionally " jarrings and bickerings " (no doubt what I have just quoted was the sequel to one of them), and always she scans them to see where she was to blame, and if she does not succeed in her quest, she still longs to do better, to take all the burden of such " jarrings," which to one less entirely loving would have been a source of grievance against him, on to her own shoulders. "Edward," she writes, "was very low this evening with neuralgia, and spoke but little and seemed easily irritated. But he was evidently suffering so much and feeling so unwell that my heart yearned for him. But I have not yet deserved the privilege of being his comforter: I never feel my own want of womanliness so much as when he is in trouble or ill. However, I wait and hope. I know it is all my fault, and the flattering tongues of my friends are very painful, as they don't suspect what a weight of guilt is under my amiable exterior. . . ."

And sometimes she had great rewards, for two days afterwards she tells how " Edward called me to pay me the money for the monthly bills of May, *which I had neglected till now*—he paid me also my own allowance, increasing it to £60. I was quite taken aback by his generosity, when I had been behaving so badly, so that I could scarcely thank him. . . . After chapel that evening Mr. Martin came in, and referred a little to going abroad. I should like it so much that I can hardly dare to think of it for fear of being disappointed, for I don't at all deserve such a pleasure. Edward spoke to me before him about something I had neglected. I almost said something about it at night, but restrained myself. I am *so* glad I did so. I drew out a plan this evening of daily duties ! . . ."

But however sorely undeserving was this miscreant of such a pleasure, she got it, and a tour in France down to the frontiers of Spain took place, the voyagers being two friends of my father, himself and my mother, who, clearly at his wish, kept a special and stupendous diary which she prefaces with a dedicatory note. " I write this diary," she says, " in the hope that it may record an improvement in my life, of which, God knows, there is only too much need"; and in it she puts down with incredible care all that interested not herself, but my father. Their sight-seeing was practically confined to churches, and under his guidance she made the most amazing series of architectural notes : you would have thought she was qualifying for a clerkship in the firm of some ecclesiastical builder. It was " churches, churches all the way " from the moment they set foot in Boulogne, where she notes the " fine Corinthian columns in the nave," having, I am sure, been instructed that very day as to what a Corinthian column was. St. Wolfran's at Abbeville follows, " flamboyant and consequently of a very rich appearance with open parapets and curving tracery." Then comes Lisieux with Norman windows in one tower and lancet windows in the other, and then this insatiable appetite for architecture devours the windows in the Cathedral of Le Mans, which (with a touch of jubilation) " puzzled even Edward to make out. The pillars round the choir with their wonderful height and the rich foliage on the capitals and the tall, pointed, stilted arches over them, with the jewelled windows above them, were one of the most striking parts of this magnificent place." Then followed the church of Notre Dame de la Couture, with no aisles, but arches spanning fourteen yards (cannot I see my father pacing them, and my mother taking down these magnificent dimensions!), and then the château at Blois. From the château they fly to the cathedral "arranged Basilica-wise," and go on to Nantes, where she and my father went out before breakfast for a "cursory view" of the cathedral supplemented by a "closer survey" directly after. But then at last, though the spirit was willing, the flesh was weak: "I was so tired and knocked up that I could not look at anything, and what I did see I could scarcely remember, so I rested all day till nearly evening, when I went to see a new church with Edward (transition between Norman and early French)," and immediately afterwards they started for Angers.

The next morning (being Sunday) they attended mass in the cathedral, went back to an English service in the hotel, and forth again to Nones, Vespers, and Compline in the cathedral, "while Mr. Walford and Mr. Martin went off by themselves" (clearly to rest). But on the way to Nones, Vespers, and Compline they "darted" into the Prefecture (Norman arches and cloisters), and after service proceeded to catalogue the sculptures on the doorway, and "then there was just time before dinner to run down to the bridge and have a look at the Loire." Next morning, "as there was a good deal to see," a fine early start was necessary, and they paid a third visit to the cathedral, as they had missed a "bénitier," "which King René brought from the East, and is made of Porphry," and went on to the church of the Holy Trinity and the cloisters and chapels of the Hospice of St. Jean, "a very curious and interesting place which I will not attempt to describe. Edward made a minute plan of the vaulting." Then they visited the wards of the hospital, and on to the museum, the art-section of which was not open, and so after a visit to the Natural History Department they went off to the Pont de Cé, four miles distant, where, as she records with a nuance of relief, "there was nothing to see but the bridge." On their return, the art-section of the museum was open, and they inspected statues and croziers and pictures. They dine at the hotel, and then leave by train for Tours (already visited), but there was just enough light to see the bridge, and go to bed in anticipation of an early start next morning to Poictiers and Bordeaux, where in the cathedral "the triforium windows were larger than those in the clerestory."

It is for the purpose of showing my mother's triumph of surrender to my father that I have extracted these notes from the first fortnight of the French tour. She obliterates herself altogether, and is concerned only with throwing her whole energy into appreciation of all that my father, not she, enjoyed. She was but twenty-one at this time, though already the mother of two sons and expectant of a third child, and in herself (her own private self, now hermetically bottled) she cared no more for aisles and triforiums than she cared for algebra. But he did, and so every day, when the sight-seeing of this Herculean holiday was closed by the impenetrable shades of night, she sat down to record what she *had* to be interested in, in order to render herself more worthy, and advance " the improvement in her life," to which the dedication of her diary aspires. That absorbing desire to be interested in what he loved was her hourly and daily aim, and these dull and touching pages are the expression of her longing to share in his appreciations. Just once or twice Minnie, the volatile one, whom she was so anxious to suppress, pops out, and with gusto but in parentheses, she records how French fisherwomen dig for eels, and how she listens to a " long quaint sermon on Patience, which was very appropriate." And I cannot acquit her of a certain demure glee when she tells how Edward fell asleep while sitting on a wall in the middle of sight-seeing. They were all dead-beat that day, but he recovered first, and went off to " catalogue " in the cathedral.

Next spring (*æt.* 22) she records a trouble about bills dated, in the depth of despair, " Ash Wednesday."

" This ought to be (and to all appearance will be) a time of great trouble and sorrow for me. I have most woefully neglected my bills, having, in spite of Edward's constant requests and my own most wretched sense of duties undone, gone on from day to day, always deceiving myself and imagining that *this* day had its own peculiar duties, and that to-morrow I would do them. The truth is, I believe, that I dreaded them. It is cowardly, I know, and now that I have done them and am going to give them to Edward this afternoon, I find they amount to over £200. What he will say I scarcely dare think, and to crown all Mamma is here, and it will grieve her terribly. If we were alone, I could bear these hours better, but to have Mamma as witness and make her so unhappy is almost intolerable. I know she takes my part, and that makes it worse still. Also of late Edward has been persuaded to take a horse on trial, and I fear that he will simply and at once throw it up. . . . What I fear most is that he will punish himself by denying himself things, and this is worse to me than anything. But I deserve it all, and must bear it. Anyhow, I never again will let my accounts get the least crooked. This I trust is final. And now I am going to keep a regular diary all through Lent, hoping that I may be able to have some true Easter joy and Easter happiness. That confidence between us may be restored, it seems as if I had to go through the valley of the shadow of death, but I have no hope without that of getting into the region of calm and peace beyond!"

She put off this confession for a couple of days yet, and with it the promised "Lenten diary" which shall make her worthy of Easter joy comes to an abrupt end. But her agony at causing him annoyance was there, and later a crystallization of her eager adaptation of herself to him. "He thinks more of little remarks, is more sensitive, more easily wounded than I am. Therefore I must not think of being at ease, but of suiting my ways to his feelings, and this without a shadow of thinking that my ways are better than his, though I like them better. . . ." Her utter abnegation of herself in the conduct of her life must have led her to precisely that conclusion. Another way would have been to have withstood him when she thought him unreasonable, to have moderated him when she thought him harsh, but with regard to him that never could have been her way : it would have been that of a totally different woman. With regard to him her mind had been made up when she was eleven years old. His work, his greatness, his untiring devotion to his ideals must be allowed to develop their full horse-power, without let or leakage from domestic disturbance. It was his way to tear along, sweeping up everything and everybody into the whirlwind of his own enthusiasms, and this she accepted and embraced. If sometimes it seemed to her that his touch was harsh and impatient, her own sweetness and her own patience were there to neutralize it. That was why they were there.

One thing alone she kept entirely outside the orbit of his influence, that part of her, namely, which she somewhere calls " the power that lies behind my will," the Director of that *vie intérieure*, which accepts no point of view except that which it dictates. It thus happened that when some fifteen years after her marriage she experienced a great spiritual crisis, she did not take her difficulties to him. No doubt, in part, that was because when she realized that her own faith in Christianity was tottering, she realized also what an unspeakable grief that revelation would be to him. But below that there was a more essential reason: she knew that his avenue of approach up which he must try to lead her back, was, though it led to the same goal, an alien ground to her. All his life his road had run on rock; never, I suppose, for a moment had he felt the smallest questioning as to the verity and validity of the Christian revelation. His faith, untroubled and fierce and fiery, could scarcely be tolerant of anything less ardent and sure than itself: doubt, in his view, partook almost of spiritual crime. . . . So, at least, I reconstruct the reason of her silence to him about that which mattered more than all the world to both of them.

My mother, throughout her life, like all very intellectual women, formed strong emotional attachments to those of her own sex. It was through friendship, she says somewhere, that love first came to her, and just at this crisis there entered into her environment a woman with whom she instantly made one of those intimate and noble friendships, not knowing, as she records, that she was the messenger. "I played with the human love I had for her, and she for me, and all the time Thou hadst sent her. . . ." As the intimacy deepened, she found that her friend knew the road which she instinctively felt must be her own, and, as by some splendid illumination, long groped for in dimness, came the light. Surely no one had ever lived a sweeter and more unselfish life than she, but all that appeared to her now to have been but a blind stumbling of steps, a haphazard goalless wandering, and it was with something of the inspired vision of the mystic that she saw then that which never afterwards, even in the darkest places (and many were dark) through which her way led her, ceased to enlighten her. "Only this I know," she wrote now, "that it is this innermost ultimate self that is filled with consuming hunger and thirst for the living Saviour. It seemed first a famine for God, simply; now I find I need a Way to Him. I linger in the holy place, and as once, for all mankind, Thou rentest the veil, so surely for each individual there comes a rending, and seeing Thee at last for their Saviour, they find that a Holy of Holies is open, yes, even to the mercy-seat of God. Therefore, Jesu, my joy, I have burned the incense of prayer before the veil dimly, with eager longing. Surely the Day of Atonement is near, nay, even is it not here? And is not the veil even now rending, and the glory of the Lord filling the house of my heart ? . . ."

But if, in this access to the spring of her spiritual life (there all the time, but now consciously reached by her, and never again quitted), my mother did not seek my father's guidance, it was by that source that she found him in a way that she had not found him yet. He had travelled there on the firm granite road, which seemed to have been hewn for him in childhood without effort of his, and which no torment of intellectual doubt had ever threatened to destroy or render impassable. She obtained then a far deeper comprehension of him as he essentially was, below his impatience and censure of frailties and childishnesses, which in her begot only an added tenderness. She had never been at one with him over such, and if she had been obliged to criticize these outlooks of his, she would have called them harsh, and he, from his standpoint, would have called her weak or over-indulgent. But now the initiation which had come to her gave her a completer comprehension of him ; her fear of him vanished altogether, and she saw that he looked towards the same centre as she, though from a different angle. But she did not, because she could not, share in his method of service. If, on his appointment to the new See of Truro, for instance, it had been she, not he, whose enthusiasm had to kindle the county into building the cathedral, not a spadeful of earth would ever have been turned in the digging of its foundations. She, to put it broadly, looked on God as a Father, he as an omnipotent King. In consequence she came to separate him, the man to whom she gave her heart's devotion, from the projects to which he gave his. No one was prouder than she when the new cathedral was consecrated for worship, but she was proud of it because it was his achievement, not because it was a cathedral. On the other hand, when Martin, her eldest son, died at Winchester, she laid him on the bosom of God with a joy that my father could never feel. His strength, which was here his weakness, cried out and rebelled: her strength accepted and welcomed.

As the years went on, and in especial when my father was appointed Archbishop, though her devotion to him could not be increased, for he had it all, the scope and scale of its working was vastly magnified. She loved and revelled in her responsibilities as mistress of the great house, serenely dispensing its hospitalities, and oiling all the machinery, so that his wheels should run without grit or hitch. She loved entertaining on a great scale, and being entertained : to meet and be in the midst of those who carried on the government of Church and State was a rich pleasure to her. The sights and shows, the debates and ceremonials, the state functions and ecclesiastical occasions, bishops and princes and prime-ministers, rulers and those in authority made a pomp and pageantry that stimulated and enchanted her. To be in the middle of it all, to know what great things were going on, and to talk to those who geared and regulated the engines was a romance in her destiny. But through it all, if my father directly needed her, or if she could have served him by some sojourn in a remote and desolate fen, she would have bounced off, in the middle of all the hum and activity, to the nearest station, and left her luggage to follow her, not with the faintest shadow of regret at what she was missing, but with an ecstasy of anticipation as to what she could do for him when she got to her mournful destination. Two things only remained to her of her own which were not his : these were her personal relation to God, and her personal relation to her children and friends. Apart from these she had absolutely no individual life of her own : she had neither artistic nor literary taste that absorbed any part of her, and any interruption to her own pursuits was to her far more important than the pursuit itself. All her enthusiasm and energy was at the service of others. Yet through it all, through all the self-abandonment with which she flung herself into the furtherance of his schemes and ideals for the Church, she cared primarily not for what they were in themselves, but for the fact that they were his. She knew that perfectly well : so also with a sense of loss and incompleteness did my father. But without her there would have been a void in his life which no one else could conceivably have filled : without her he would have been maimed and crippled.

There were times when the lights were low, times when the whirling wheels slowed down and halted, and it was then chiefly that she was prey to fear, that life-long arch-enemy of her soul. These times were when my father was evidently overtaxed with stress of work, or when, even more markedly, the stress was over, and he in holiday-time hobbled out of the shafts, and felt the reaction from his stupendous activities. Then, more completely than ever, but with some sort of enslavement, she was his, for her anxiety and fear chained her to him in his dark places not for his enlightenment, but for her eclipse. By some sort of nervous metabolism in the dwindling

MOTHER

of elasticity and rebound which even in the most vital is a necessary limitation of middle life, she made his depressions hers and converted them into fear. Those glooms, which from the early years had been a malady of his, were not very frequent, and as he grew older became rarer and less opaque, but now she seemed to catch from them some infection, which " came out " in her in an increase of anxiety about him, which did not wholly lift when he recovered his strength and spring. Her anxiety about him became chronic with her, couched in the shadow and ever ready to pounce on her with claws and teeth, if the smallest ailment attacked him. The acutest observer, I fancy, would never have conjectured how deep that anxiety was. She smothered the symptoms which might have betrayed its presence: only very intimately, as to her diary, she acknowledged it. Even when my father was well and vigorous, she never quite let herself push off in confidence, but was always on the look-out for shoals ahead.

During the summer of 1896 this chronic fear and apprehension had become much more than an external enemy to be bludgeoned into submission. It had stolen in now and sat by the hearth, and there was no getting rid of it. But I do not believe that there was anything premonitory about it; at the most her subconscious self had seen a little more clearly than her reasonable, conscious self, and drew conclusions from what it already knew, not from what it anticipated. What appears to be prophetic is almost always not prophetic at all, but merely derived from a more sensitive appreciation of the past.

Fear was no new thing to her, but never had the assault of it been so fiercely beleaguering, and in her diary hitherto, she had done no more than allude to it with a word of self-contempt at her weakness. But now she analysed and dwelt on it, as if to fortify herself by facing it, or at least by direct scrutiny to see what it was. "Fear," she wrote now, "my deadliest and most constant foe, coming most as anxiety as to the health of my immediate belongings. . . . There seems a hastiness and impatience of mind and heart: it is like panic taking possession of me, a sort of demon of fright. As I write Dr. Douglas Powell is seeing Edward, and of course I am rather jumpy. I don't really at bottom think there is anything radically wrong, but I fear. . . . One has, I think, to determine to behave with courage, as if one was not afraid, whatever one is feeling."

Now this medical examination of my father

was made in view of a terrific programme that had been arranged for the visit he was to pay to the Anglican Church of Ireland in September. The report of Dr. Douglas Powell was that his heart was weak in power, but how lightly both he and a colleague regarded that may be seen from the fact that they neither wanted him to give up his tour nor suggested any curtailment of his engagements. They did not think that the programme would be likely to overtax his strength, nor did they anticipate any breakdown. They suggested that he should rest before and after meals, and my mother notes that " he is furious, and won't." The verdict should have been reassuring, but my mother found no relief from the fear that " lay like lead on her heart."

And then there rose high her courage and resource. Her reasonable mind told her that she was unreasonable, she held tight to that, and easily conjectured a cause for her apprehensions. Her depression and fears were due to these August heats following on the sedentary months in London, and she must diet herself with gritty and unpalatable biscuits. . . . She deliciously records in her diary the rules she made for herself and quite as deliciously the breaking of them. How one day she ate what she liked at dinner, and finished with two strictly forbidden peaches. And then she gets humorously disgusted, not so much with her " greediness " (as she firmly terms it), but with her thinking at all about the privations she has ordained for herself. " I am getting to let my thoughts *dwell* on dieting, and of *all* stupid subjects ! Do it, and leave it behind——" And off she goes (precisely as she did when she was first married) into a scrutiny of the calls and interruptions, of which during all these years at Lambeth her life really consisted. At the beck and whistle of so many for whose summons she would whisk aside whatever occupation held her, she had in truth no private life of her own, and yet out of her very self-abnegation, she tries to carve a passage where a more complete unselfishness can enter. " What I need so greatly is loving energy. . . . Surely God means me largely to look for and wisely to see what my real duties are, and perform them greedily, as opportunities for service. . . . I must be glad of all the calls, and not silence them as quickly as possible." And then without pause she gives a despairing wail over the stupid subject, which she had resolved never to allude to again. " Scarcely any loss of weight. I AM going to be rigid this week."

So in September my father and she went off to

Ireland, and days, prodigious with sermons and ceremonies, and warming and glorious to his heart, flew by. My mother confided to her diary that the Archbishop of Dublin was a slave-driver, and that they were being hunted (which from the list of my father's engagements seems a well-warranted statement); she confided to it also that her fear never left her. It grew on her like a panic; if he blew his nose the cold hands clutched her; a horrid access of fear seized her because he settled on a day of boisterous wind to walk back three miles from the church he had been visiting. Yet all the time my father's health seemed remarkably good, there was no question of his not being able to stand the strain of these busy days, for he appeared to enjoy them hugely, and to gather speed from his going. And the tour came to an end, and having spent a day at Carlisle they arrived on a Saturday evening at Hawarden. My father sat up late that night in vigorous conclave with Mr. Gladstone, next morning he attended early communion in church, and walked there again for Matins at eleven o'clock. The service had hardly begun, when he sank forward and all was over. She to whom, at the age of eleven, he had written his first love-poem, was beside him still.

CHAPTER II

MY mother had no moment of struggle or rebellion. She accepted what had happened as an inscrutable and perfect decree of God, but it stunned her: she looked out on to an inconceivable emptiness. The object of her life's devotion, he who for more than forty years had never been out of the focus of her service, had passed from the sight of her steadfast eyes. In all the flood of decisions to be made, urgent businesses to be done, and in the winding up of the two big houses, she did all that was required, but in some kind of trance. My father had no private residence of his own to leave her, for though he had thought of repurchasing a small family estate in Yorkshire, which in time of financial trouble a hundred years ago had been sold, nothing had come of it, and it was necessary to clear out of Lambeth and Addington as soon as possible, not only for the convenience of his successor, but in order to cut down without delay the expenses of such upkeep. It was impossible

MARY BENSON.
(Aged 19.)

that she should solve the problem of where her future home was to be at once, and as my sister Maggie was to spend the winter again in Egypt, it was settled that my mother and her great friend Lucy Tait, who for the last six years had lived with us, should go there also. Simultaneously, my brother Hugh developed an acute attack of rheumatism, which disclosed a chronic condition below, and he was forbidden to pass the winter in London, where he was working at the Eton Mission. So Hugh joined the party, which I was to follow as soon as possible.

For the present I was tied here, for my father had only a few months before finished the work which had been his characteristic leisure-pastime for thirty years, namely a book on the Life and Times of St. Cyprian, Archbishop of Carthage. For years on holidays the "Cyprian box," with manuscript and mammoth authorities, had travelled with him; now its re-writing and appendices were done, and the final proofs of it must be passed for press. These were now being read by his friend Mr. Alexis Larpent, who had long been working for my father on points of verification and such, but Mr. Larpent refused to assume responsibility for the remainder without the sanction of one of the family, and so night after December night he and I used to sit in some echoing half-dismantled room at Lambeth, while Mr. Larpent explained to me why he proposed to omit a reference to Plotinus or insert a passage from St. Augustine. Of all these things I knew nothing whatever, but I had to give my decision whether or no this should be done or the other left undone, and often I felt myself casting a glance of deprecating apology towards the image of my father at the idea of my correcting his Cyprian for him. . . .

So for a month after the Egyptian party had left, I continued living in the huge mournful house so lately humming with central and superb activities, while such furniture as we desired to keep drifted away for indefinite storage: the supervision of this occupied the day, until Mr. Larpent arrived at nightfall. Carpets were rolled up and sideboards shrouded and a freshness of colour behind removed pictures made squares and oblongs on the dismantled walls. My mother could not bear to part with anything that was intimately associated with my father, and shelves full of folio editions of early Christian saints were stored in the cupboards of great Victorian mahogany wardrobes, which had formed part of the furnishing of their first house. Rooms full of sheeted forms and creaking staircases were no longer lit, and by the illumination of a candle placed handy by the caretaker whose steps then retreated to an infinite distance, tapping in diminuendo down the endless corridors, I used to find my way eerily to bed. Since I was sixteen this had been so splendid and beloved a home, full of budding interests and ravenous eagernesses, and now it lay moribund, with the last drops of its life-blood, as far as our family affairs went, dripping from it. Everything was over, and nothing new had yet begun.

From that sense of emptiness and desolation, I could begin to guess with what sense of a full page turned in the middle of a sentence, to find overleaf the sentence unfinished and the book done, my mother a month ago had gone forth to meet life again. The space that my father had filled in the lives of any of us was not a hundredth part of his relation to her: to him and his life and his service and his needs she had been anchored for many more years than any of her children had lived, and that with a tautness of devotion that only her great heart could comprehend. All that was over, and over, too, when she looked towards her own life in the future, were the splendours and activities of her worldly position.

My consciousness of what the break meant to her was but dim and veiled, much like the bleared light of the morning when I heard the great gate of Morton's tower clang behind me, and knew it to be shut for ever on home. And not with any real knowledge did I appreciate what her emptiness must have been until, on a windy day of spring at Lamb House, I read the pages of her diary of those days, which told of that and of the unquenchable spirit of hers which by degrees rose up again within her.

It was as if some earthquake had occurred, some elemental upheaval and tearing, that separated from her an entity which had once been hers. It made a rending of her personality; part dwelt still on the severed island, the rest of her on the mainland from which by this cataclysm it had been severed. Between those sundered parts of her flowed the impassable sea. By some sort of wireless telegraphy only, through the medium of the ether which lay over island and sea and mainland alike, could she establish communication. And the ether was the will of God. . . .

The first message that came to her, but too intimate to quote, was when she knelt by my father's coffin in front of the altar of Canterbury Cathedral, and by his side on the morning of his funeral received the Communion. It was a conviction so real that it became to her not a conviction alone, but an event: she felt herself choosing him out of all the world to be eternally hers, and spoke of the rapture of his actual presence with a free heart.

And so in his death she came nearer to him than in all the years before, full as they were of devotion and dedication. That illumination of my father's presence, which never afterwards was quenched, was her lighthouse. It burned always, though its ray, as could not but happen, often shone only on an opacity of blinding fog, and there follow, in her diary, weeks of silence. She had to build again and to wait, in order to find herself. For there is no illumination of the spirit (except perhaps the final freedom of it) which is not followed by the darkness which its dazzling has made, and out of that blindness which succeeds the light, she was groping in despair, as she regained herself, for the stones of the structure which had been thrown and disjected in ruin about her, but which somehow must be fitted into the very foundations of the temple that was to be built of them. She recorded later on the process of that rebuilding. But it was long before she broke the silence.

"Lord God, make me strong and of a good courage. All the beauty of our past life together, the home we made, the dignity and glory of it, the fellowship, the humour, the conspiracies, the discussions, the beating, fervent, keen, pulsating life, the splendid web which Thou gavest us to weave—all this is over. With one touch Thou calledst him home, and it has fallen to pieces round me. Give me strength and power to be still and see what Thou wilt do. . . ."

"I seem to have been living in the past three weeks in the land of utter dreaminess and confusion, and I hope light is beginning to dawn. 'All over, all over,' rings in my ears, and I don't find anything inside me except the habits of life. . . . For it is not as if the children were to be brought up. One might then feel helpless enough, and out of heart enough, but life would respond to the call. . . . This dull heavy nothingness, this ceasing of every stimulus, and this terrible inner sense that all my life, all these years, was derived from and in answer to distinct, never-ceasing claims seem to kill me. There is nothing within, no power, no love, no desire, no initiative: he had it all, and his life entirely dominated mine. Good Lord, give me a personality, a scorn of small petty indulgences. Let me live to Thy works, and Thee, to everything beautiful and desirable, and to all interests, to all knowledge, to all wisdom, and beyond all and in all and through all to Thyself. Thy love. . . .

" The sacrifice of God is a troubled spirit. The offering of a free heart. . . .

" Now all is over and nothing is required of me but to enjoy, and that I can't do. I feel exactly like a string of beads, always on one string, worn, carried about till they seemed as if they had some real coherence. In a moment the string was cut; they rolled to all corners of the room, a necklace for glory and beauty no longer, but just scattered beads. Who will string my life together once more ?

" The Vision of Personality. . . . It seemed like a deep burning fire down in the heart of God. How to connect this with finding myself ? I feel as if I had led a superficial life so long, not wilfully or wrongly exactly. But united as I was with so dominant a personality as Edward, and being, especially of late, so often in such anxiety about him, combined with the tremendous claims of the position, how was I to find myself ? I don't say it mightn't have been possible to a greater or truer or more virile nature, but to mine so hard that I don't blame myself overmuch. But now

I must [find myself], and my first despair is that I have fallen to pieces since Edward left me. I seem to have been only a service of respondings, and no *core*. But there must be a core, and it is in God. In quietness and confidence shall be my strength. I think I must have wanted *my own courage,* now I want God's strength, which can never fail, but which cannot be granted to the human spirit unless it rests on Him.

" I lived hastily through the hours in response to immediate claims, and in the intervals I did what I liked. I have never had time to be responsible for my own life. In a way, I feel more grown up now than I have ever felt before. Strange, when for the first time in my fifty-five years I am answerable to nobody. No one has a right to question my actions, and I can do as I like. What a tremendous choice! Little enough in the eyes of the world how one more widow who has to come down from a really high position pitches her small tent.

" O God, open my eyes that I may see the beauty and loveliness of this glorious creation of Thine which Thou hast given me, that in Thy light, gazing with unobscured vision into the eternal world, I may make the offering of a free heart and receive from Thy hands that which is my own. I must wrestle day by day, never leaving off, till 'through faith I see him face to face.'

"I can offer my own poor offering, not gifts and powers and influence and career, but just what comes to me daily: discomforts, anxieties, fears, disabilities. I believe in my soul that they will be an offering of sweet savour."

Here then are the courage and the faith and the humanity with which she met the break-up of her career of service: no mere description of them, but the living flame itself in the light of which, looking out on to nothingness, she faced the featureless perspective of the future. It was all hidden away out of sight of daily intercourse and intimacy, and in it there is not one touch of self-pity or hint of resignation, that most deadly of Christian virtues. She suffered no such to come near her (for how she hated them!), and to all appearance, even to eyes most scrutinizing and loving, she seemed to be building and reconstructing again with eagerness and glee. It is just for this reason that I print these secret confessions, for they show with how brave a face " nothingness " can be met. She appeared to suffer no loss of humour, of pleasure, of entranced interest in life. Was there ever anyone so firmly rooted, and so sweetly flowering?

I rejoined them at Luxor, and plunged into the exuberance of their occupations. My sister had started again the excavations which she had been making for the last two winters, by the horse-shoe lake at Karnak, and day by day an imposing procession of large white donkeys cavalcaded to the Temple of Mut. There was Maggie jingling with bags of piastres for pay-day, with her donkey-boy carrying a tea-basket for picnic on the site, and my mother, following a little more sedately with Lucy Tait, would be quite unable to resist the importunities of the sellers of small antique objects.

"English gentleman, he offer me a pound for this scarab," called one of these perjured vendors, "but I said 'no.' I keep it for you, lady."

My mother cast a longing eye at a forged scarab.

"Certainly not," she said. "Give it to the English gentleman for a pound."

"But I give it you for three shillings," explained the perjured one.

Shrill cries for Maggie, who cantered back.

"Oh, Maggie, isn't it rather attractive?" said my mother.

Maggie gave it a contemptuous glance.

"Forgery: mafish, mish-mish," said she

severely. " Not a pound nor three shillings nor a penny. Go away ! "

" Then the Princess will buy it of me for two shillings ? " said the vendor, still hopeful, and approaching Lucy.

" I'm not a Princess," said Lucy. " I'm a plain miss. Take it away."

And my mother, resigned but yearning, put up her parasol to shield temptation from her.

Then sometimes as we drew near to the scene of the digging, it would be clear that some excitement was on the bubble, and cries of " Antica ! " which indicated that some find had been made came across the horse-shoe lake, and Maggie's money-bags, as she slapped her donkey into a swifter canter, jingled more loudly, and the tea-cups in the basket played livelier castanets with each other, as Mohammed panted after her. Perhaps this was a red-letter day, when the Saite head of a priestess, which now, gravely smiling, watches me as I write, was disinterred in the trench that we were digging along the temple wall. Beyond was the outer court where masons were busy with cranes and mortar, raising and cementing together the pieces of fallen statues of Pasht, and to right and left of that were the priests' chambers, which once had guarded the

secrets of some remote initiation, and there was Maggie, priestess of the new era that unveiled the old, and Mohammed behind her, plying the flywhisk, as, after a joyful inspection of the new find, the Saite head or the Scribe of Akknaton, she dispensed the wages of the week, and refreshed herself with glances at the trove, and sips of tea.
. . . And my mother was there, intent on finding out at once and exactly in her guide-book who Akenaton was, and being thrilled in ascertaining that he was a notable heretic who worshipped the orb or disc of the sun rather than the sun itself, and ready to maintain against all-comers that it was not at all the same thing. For myself I had undertaken to make a plan to scale of the temple and was busy with strings and measures and pegs driven in at corners of walls (the pegs invariably came out, when for purposes of accuracy you stretched the string, and made pleasant parabolas in the air). Then the amiable M. Le Grain, director of excavations, would hear of the find as he superintended the diggings in the Hall of Columns at Karnak, and ride over to see it, and propose to remove it to his store-house for safety. Expostulations ensued from Maggie, who wanted to take it back to the hotel at Luxor and gloat . . . and M. Le Grain was indulgent, and said

that it should certainly be as she wished. Hugh would join the archæologists of his family, with the spoils of his day's shooting, two quail and a jackal, and at sunset the enriched procession returned to Luxor, for there was the Scribe on a trolly with the spoils of the chase sacrificially disposed at his feet, and Mohammed told my mother the strange story of the golden dahabeah that cruised at midnight when the moon was full on the horse-shoe lake. Laden it was with pearl and amber, and heaped with jewels, and all the richness of it was the property of anyone who could set foot on its ivory deck without word or exclamation. But so rich, sumptuous, and glittering were its treasures that none could board it without an ejaculation of delight that its store was his. Then, on his astonished cry, the golden dahabeah would sink, and he would find himself immersed in the horse-shoe lake. . . . When Mohammed told that tale to those of his own sex, the dahabeah was peopled with unveiled houris of seductive loveliness and of no great moral integrity, but that was not polite for female ears.

Another day would be given to an expedition across the Nile, with lunch in the desert or on the terrace at Deir-el-Bahari, and a game of knuckle-bones for dessert. That was my mother's despair: the backs of her small plump hands could never catch the hail of the descending bones which she had tossed up. "But I will do it," she said. "I am just as clever as any of you. Oh, Fred, why am I so stupid?" Then in the evenings we played the old silly games, making poems, and words out of words, and drawing each other. Lucy, unable to think of rhymes and falling fast asleep, would wake suddenly, and say to my mother, "Ben, isn't it time for you to go to bed?" And Ben told her that she was still dreaming, and that it wasn't time to wake up. . . . Mixed with these activities was the ineradicable habit of the family to be engaged on literary production. What Hugh's work was I cannot remember, but he did a great deal of writing, and Maggie was busy with notes of her excavations and stories about animals, and I was romancing about the Greek War of independence. So my mother's rôle of General Auditor to her children's works was no sinecure. She threw herself into everything, and her apparent effortlessness and spontaneity of interest were the true measure of her courage, for all the time there was going on within her, as her diary recorded, that ceaseless struggle to emerge from nothingness. Hugh left the party for a tour in Palestine on his way back to England, having first hoisted a warning flag of what was to come, by catching a severe feverish chill. But that passed off, and away he went, and for the next four months life became a mere nightmare. While my mother was at Assouan for a few days, Maggie followed Hugh's example, but instead of getting the better of her chill, it virulently got the better of her. One lung became affected, and then the other, and before long she was seriously though not dangerously ill. While she was in this state, I had a curious psychical experience.

The doctor used now to see her three times a day, in the morning, after lunch, and in the evening, and I always waited for the mid-day report before going back to the temple where work still went on. On one such day I was sitting in the garden at Luxor at the back of the hotel: in front of me was a broad sweep of sandy path, and beyond that a small raised terrace on to which the long windows of the dining-room and drawing-room opened. A flight of three or four steps led down to the sandy path. After waiting a little, I saw the doctor come out of the drawing-room, looking pleased and rubbing his hands together. Instead of walking down the steps he jumped down on to the path, and coming towards me said, "Well, we've found what we wanted." I then instantly became aware that his appearance and his speech were a hallucination: there was no doctor there at all. When, some few minutes later he did come out, his report was graver than usual, and he said nothing about having found what he wanted, because he was not looking for anything. The whole affair was at present quite meaningless.

That afternoon I did not go to the temple, but remained with my mother, who was in the greatest anxiety about Maggie. In the hope of comforting her a little, but partly in order to put on record this odd illusion of mine, I told her of it, and said, "I believe it will happen: it was of the quality of real things." But the next day passed and Maggie developed pleurisy, and the morning after my servant told me, as I was dressing, that the doctor wished to speak to me. His news was that my sister had this liquid round her lungs, and probably a tapping-operation must be done that day. He explained that the tapping in itself was nothing: the question was what they would find. The liquid might be clear, in which case it could be drawn off and she would experience considerable relief; it might, on the other hand, be found to be purulent, and her condition must then be regarded as extremely serious. . . .

The tapping took place that day after lunch, and I happened, waiting for his report, to sit just in the same place in the garden where, forty-eight hours before, I had seen the phantasmal doctor. Presently he came out of the drawing-room window, and walked across the terrace, looking pleased and rubbing his hands together. Instead of using the steps, he jumped down on to the path, and came towards me. " Well, we've found what we wanted " were his exact words.

For some days after that Maggie held her own. Then quite suddenly one Sunday morning, her heart gave out, and she had an attack of syncope. We were all sent for, and as I entered the room the doctor took me aside a moment. " She can't recover," he said. My mother was there already, and as we waited together by her bed we were witnesses of a soul praying itself back into life.

Maggie was lying quite flat; the pillows had been taken from under her head, the bed had been moved out into the middle of the room, and all doors and windows were wide, so that the maximum of air might reach her. Her eyes were closed, her face and hands were bluish in tinge. And then in a voice faint, but perfectly firm, she began to pray aloud. " Father, make me better. Quickly make me better," she said over and over again, " Father, make me better. . . ." After a few minutes she said, " I'm a little better," and again and over and over again she repeated that one sentence, as if she knocked on a door and would not cease till it was opened to her. Another ten minutes, perhaps, passed, and the door swung on its hinges. She grew quieter. " I'm better, she said, " I'm better," and thus from the very valley of death she turned back and came to us.

It was already growing very hot at Luxor, and some ten days afterwards the doctor sanctioned her being moved, and she was carried, mattresses and all, just as she lay, on to a Nile tourist steamer bound for Cairo. From Cairo we were all going for a week to Helouan. But already, had we known it, I had begun to take an active part in this nightmare of illness, and I did it in very effective manner. During Maggie's convalescence, the heat during the day being too great for riding, I got a canoe, and used to paddle up the Nile to some convenient sandbank, and spend the afternoon swimming and basking on the sandbank and swimming again when toasted. From one of these expeditions I came back with a notable headache, and went to the doctor, who asked me what I had been doing. When he looked at his clinical thermometer which registered a few degrees of fever, he very naturally told me that I had got a touch of sun, which was no more than I deserved, and that for the next few days I must keep quiet and go slow. I obeyed and did not consult him again, but noticed that a touch of sun produced a queer feeling of unreality: sensations and actions seemed to belong to somebody else, not me. All one saw or heard appeared rather unusual: one evening, for instance, the night before the departure for Cairo, when my mother and I were sitting in the garden, a sudden wind got up and set the date-palms in the garden rattling their top-knots of fibrous foliage. But they seemed far more like curious gaunt beings, waving their arms in mystical lamentation. I really was not sure whether they were trees or not.

There were still a few odds and ends to finish up with the packing of our antiquities from the excavations, and I had settled to remain at Luxor a couple of days yet, and then take the swifter post-boat for Cairo, which would arrive there a few hours before the tourist boat; I could thus pleasantly meet them on the quay at Cairo. The sense of unreality still persisted; but it was odd rather than disagreeable; I felt drowsy and light-headed together and wonderfully remote. I did not feel ill, only odd, and so one day, the ninth after that on which the sun had touched me, it seemed best to have some curried chicken for lunch, by way of strengthening my contact with the world. But the morning after I did feel ill, and stopped in my cabin, but managed toast and butter for breakfast. . . . And then all at once it struck me that there was something really wrong, and I telegraphed from some stopping place to the doctor at Helouan, who was in any case to meet the tourist boat with my sister on board, asking him if he could meet the post-boat first. We got to Cairo that afternoon, and he came on board, took my temperature and, after hearing my history, asked me what I had eaten that day and the day before. This seemed to interest him very much, but when I told him about curried chicken and crisp toast he looked worried. He then announced that I must lie quite still while he got an ambulance, on which he proposed to take me through Cairo and out to Helouan. . . . At that I felt vastly intelligent, and asked him if I had got typhoid.

He told me that I must behave as if I had, and wrote a note for my mother to be given her on the arrival of the tourist boat. Then the ambulance came, and off we went, and my mother a few hours later was met with the encouraging news that I had been taken off the boat on a stretcher and was being personally conducted to Helouan by Dr. Page May. Typhoid it was, for my guess had been perfectly correct, and I herewith claim a niche in the temple of fame, for having continued to partake of ordinary adult diet, curried chicken and toast and all, up to the middle of the second week of that disease without any disastrous sequel. For a brief but sensational period then I held the stage, and Maggie who was making a marvellous recovery became quite a subsidiary character, for she had only one trained nurse and I had two, and the chart of my thermometer, which outlined a row of eminent and precipitous summits, was the centre of interest. Then those peaks began to dwindle into mere highlands, and the highlands of this admirable chart declined to sea-level again, and it looked as if the family were awakening from this nightmare of existence. Not at all! Soon came a day when, after Maggie had just had her evening temperature taken (we seemed to do nothing but take temperatures), an idle discussion took place between her and my mother and Lucy Tait, as to how convenient it was that on a very hot day, such as this, the clever blood managed not to get heated. To illustrate this, Lucy proceeded to take her temperature, and the clever blood said that it was 102°. So she went to bed, and typhoid duly declared itself, and she became the centre of interest, and my night nurse, since nobody cared about me any longer, was transferred to her. She grew steadily and terribly worse: her sister, Mrs. Davidson, and Bishop Davidson of Winchester were sent for, and for many hours her life hung twirling on a thread that just did not break. Then she, like Maggie, wheeled round from the gates of death. One parting shot the fierce Egyptian gods of destruction discharged at us, for when I went for a few days of change to the Mena Hotel by the Pyramids, I nearly stepped on a black cobra, neatly coiled on the floor of the billiard room.

So the spring of 1897 was not a very recuperative season. We had left England in search of health for my sister, and in order to get my mother away from the closing of that book of the past, into fresh scenes and new interests. New interests there undoubtedly were: these, thrillingly and absorbingly vivid, had centred round the question as to which of the party, this child of hers or that, or her dearest friend, was to stop behind in an Egyptian cemetery, or whether we were all—one after the other—to do so. But whereas each of us in turn had a remission from anxiety (for when you are so extremely unwell as we all were, it is quite impossible to care what happens to yourself or anybody else), she alone faced for months the stress and tension of the nightmare. Not a pang of it was spared her, for sixteen consecutive weeks one or other of those most dear to her, in her stricken bereavement, hung on the edge of a crumbling cliff. And, as always, when her need was the greatest, her courage burned the brightest. For four months some cliff toppled towards collapse, and all the time she watched and she prayed and was steadfast. . . . Her diary here is almost blank, but one thought touched on six months before emerges again at the end: " These visitations of God bear fruit in the soul. But the soul must dwell in peace, and let the fruit ripen."

CHAPTER III

THE plagues of Egypt being past, the Egyptian party composedly tottered to various parts of Europe. As Maggie had not died of syncope she went to Aix for rheumatic reasons; I to Athens and, on the way home, to Capri; while my mother and Lucy returned to England, and pending a habitation, stayed at Farnham Castle with Bishop Davidson, now Archbishop of Canterbury, and found Beth among those who welcomed them. Beth (it is with difficulty that I remember she was Elizabeth Cooper) had gone as nursery-maid to my grandmother at the age of fifteen, and after nursing her family, had reverted to my mother and been nurse to all of us; now she was in her eightieth year, upright and bright-eyed, and knowing no rule of life except love. And Beth wanted her children to come home again after these disastrous holidays and "have a bit of peace and quietness."

That was precisely what my mother wanted too, and when I got back from the south in July, she had settled on Winchester as her home. The house she had taken was early Georgian, spacious enough to hold the family reunited in holiday-time, and to me, at any rate, who was to be of the permanent party there, quite adorable. It would be comfortable and cosy and secure (and none of us just then had much gusto for adventure, after the Egyptian experiences); there was a sense of humdrum content in the mellowed bricks of the trim enclosed garden, of permanence in the pinnacles and towers of the cathedral which overlooked it. After the hazardous and diseased pilgrimage among the Pharaohs, homeless and hotelled, here was an *angulus terræ* again, with the Penates ready to come out of their storage and the Lares lazily to settle themselves round a quiet hearth. There were golf-links, there was the river Itchen, there was a County Club; the æsthetic eye could feast on tiled house-roofs and green valleys and the surge of windy downs, and all would be an anæsthetic that produced a pleasant dozing under the guise of mild and absorbing activities. So, during a particularly hot August we settled in, and van after van continued to arrive with furniture and early Christian Fathers, and long after the house seemed as full as it could hold, a line of immense mahogany wardrobes, and a small billiard table, and a two-manual organ, and a seated statue of Rameses the Great, stood in a *queue* down St. Thomas's Street insisting on admittance. The grey parrot (Matilda), knowing that all this pushing and pulling and growing red in the face was done in order to amuse her, kept on pulling corks to remind us that we were thirsty, and blowing her nose (rudely and vulgarly) to indicate that she was well aware that I had a cold in the head, and the green parrot (Joey) bit the foreman of the Bedford Pantechnicon for saying " Poor Polly " with a finger inserted in his cage, and Taffy, the Welsh collie, helped us all very much by lying in the gangway of the hall and growling, and Maggie's Persian cat, in this general reunion, smelled well-known objects with purring recognition. When the confusion was at its height, and the drawing-room entirely congested with furniture, a Canon of the cathedral thought it would be nice to call on us. I did not hear the announcement of his entry, because I was playing the piano in order to amuse Joey, who was perched on my shoulder and was loudly screaming. So the Persian cat, which he had tried to caress, scratched him, and Taffy very rudely bit him. Then Joey, on my shoulder, began to dance a strange Brazilian minuet, to indicate that we were no longer alone, and so I came round the corner of a bookcase and gave the Canon tea. He was a little faint, and I don't wonder. . . .

All that autumn it looked as if Winchester was to prove the final berth into which the storm-tossed family had been towed. How pleasant to hang, like the ripening plums on the garden wall, till one after the other, in some uncontemplated future, we dropped softly off the stem! And, in the meantime, everything was new and queer and small and cosy. Winchester seemed to combine the advantages of being a turmoil of entrancing, infinitesimal interests with complete leisure, and the " society," as a caller pointed out to my mother, was " so very varied." " There is the Close, Mrs. Benson; there is the County; there is the College; there is the Military. It is quite a centre!" So, indeed, it was: too far from London to have its life suburbanly sucked out of it, it turned quietly about on its own axis, like some little independent moon, borrowing its light, perhaps, from suns that wheeled about interplanetary space, but conscious of its own centrality like every other provincial nucleus, mediæval in its setting and middle-aged in its actors. To be sure, there was no great stir or fermentation to excite the vat and set it bubbling, but which of us just then desired anything more than to be let alone ? To judge by recent experience, events were invariably disagreeable ; a truce to events !

But better even than the drowsy security of the place was the fact that at first it seemed to suit Maggie. For six months she got steadily stronger, and though my mother was conscious of a growing dullness, and a growing deadness, it was sufficient for her that Maggie prospered, and negotiations were set on foot to buy the house and settle here, and die and be buried. . . . After the screwed-up tension of Egypt, mere eventlessness seemed in itself an exquisite employment, and, besides, we were already getting busy again in our own ways. Maggie, making the most, as she always did, of gathering energy, was fathoms deep in writing an account of the excavations, and every time she went through the hall there was the stimulus of the rose-granite statue of Rameses the Great, the cast of the Scribe of Akknaton, which the museum at Gizeh had claimed, and the Saite head and a limestone Sphinx, and statuettes of kings and priests to keep her zeal alive. And from Egypt she turned to " her " philosophy, now very slowly, very carefully, beginning to record itself in the book published many years later, *A Venture of Rational Faith*. Lucy Tait had her district in Lambeth to visit every week, and at home her constant companionship with my mother; while I seemed to be urgently employed over agreeable pursuits and diversions. Winchester, in fact, became a rush of pleasant minutenesses, and at Christmas came Arthur and Hugh, and once more the long evenings saw us furiously engaged in word-games and arguments and caricatures. And Taffy used to find so many friends to talk to in the High Street that sometimes his family was unable to wait for him, and when he came home the front-door would be shut. So Taffy told his trouble to his special policeman, who rang the bell for him, and one of Taffy's servants opened the door for him, and he came in, still rather agitated, to receive the congratulations of his family on his cleverness. . . .

But as the spring days began to lengthen, there grew some strange sense of impermanence and unreality. Nobody talked of it yet; it was like an unexplained shadow lying across a patch of sunlight, which everyone knew to be there and pointedly disregarded, and the shadow was this. Such life as that which my mother was now leading had been to her before no more than the diversion of her rare leisure : now there was for her nothing except leisure, and how it wearied her! The economy of this small establishment was all there was of domestic duty, whereas before she had the complete control of two very large houses, and even that had to be fitted into spare fragments and half-sheets of her time, so that she might be always free for my father's calls upon her. With his death had come not only the emptiness caused by his loss, but now, when she had to make her own life, the emptiness of having nothing that she need do. It was not that she had any less zest for the affairs and interests of her family, but that there was no other zest. She had foreseen that this must be so in the early days, but she had not foreseen—her courage and her eagerness inhibited it—that it was when she had to set about making a life for herself, the full perception of the blank would smite her. Most of all did this burden of nothingness weigh her down when she returned to Winchester from some stay in London. The old entrancing life, which for her was over, still foamed and bubbled, and she realized that she who had been in the very centre of it all must stand aside behind the barrier that excluded the general public, and at the most intelligently watch the clashings and the crossings of the loom at the centre of which she had once sat and served in the weavings of my father's work. And she saw with a regret that was unavoidable that her devotion had been given solely to his convenience and not to his work itself, the thing for which he lived. She had been Martha, she told herself, not Mary, and she ached with the sense of her past inadequacies, not seeing, in her search for an unattainable, that she had to choose one service or the other. . . . And then came her return to Winchester (already to her a stagnancy and a backwater, instead of a peace-pool), and learned our news: the wife of a master at the College had left cards, and Taffy was quite well, but couldn't remember where he had buried his bone two days ago, and had frenziedly dug up all the dahlias in order to discover it, and I had played golf twice yesterday. Maggie had gone for a drive, and that was all. . . . It was very nice as a diversion, a game after dinner, but oh, for the intense and splendid affairs that had once marched along with banners and bugles. Most of all she yearned to be wanted, and all of us who wanted her so much and so much got her, could not conceivably give her the sense of being instantly and imperiously demanded. She longed to surrender herself, and in this ceasing of the call for her surrender it was inevitable that she should find not a victory but a defeat.

Then, too, all her children were now grown up, and, as was natural, we were all developing on our own lines. She would have been the first to lament any want of development (that would have been more tragic yet), but she longed to have someone dependent on her for his work. That could not be; she could not help Arthur with his boarding-house at Eton, nor Maggie with her philosophy, nor me with the Princess Sophia, nor Hugh in his curacy at Kemsing; none of us could urgently want her like that.

Especially she realized this during the spring, when Hugh felt that he must leave Kemsing and submit himself to some more disciplined spiritual rule. She could neither help nor hinder: his conscience was adult and master in its house, and she could only laugh when Hugh, humorous even in the most soul-vexing questions, sketched the life at Kemsing under his friend the Rector, in whose luxurious house he lived. The Rector's visiting in his parish, Hugh declared, consisted in taking an afternoon drive in a landau with a pair of high-stepping horses. Sometimes the Rector would see a labourer working at the

[Photo: *Hills & Saunders.*

MARY BENSON.
(Aged 30.)

road-side, and leaning over the side of the landau would bawl out to him that he had observed his absence from church last Sunday, and hoped it would not occur again. Then he would doze a little as they bowled along, and they returned to the Rectory for a hot, comfortable tea, after which Hugh would get on with the pantomime he was writing for the school-children to act at Christmas: the organist composed music for his lyrics. If a new song was complete, the Rector faintly protesting, was easily induced to leave the composition of his sermon, and join in the chorus.

After an excellent dinner they played whist, and a glass of whisky and soda preceded retirement, and loud laughter from the Rector would indicate that he had found an apple-pie bed. . . . This was all busy and agreeable, thought Hugh, but not spiritual, and in a great hurry, like everybody else in the family except Maggie, he made arrangements for joining Canon Gore's House of the Resurrection at Mirfield. As this implied leaving the Diocese of Canterbury, he went to tell Archbishop Temple about it, who told him to get back to his work, and they both appeared to have sadly lost their tempers. But my mother induced Hugh to behave rather more filially to the Head of his Church, and it was amicably arranged that he should go to Mirfield as a probationer, without taking permanent vows. Beth disapproved of this step quite as strongly as the Archbishop had done, for she had realized that the House of the Resurrection was a communistic body, and that none of the brethren had any property of his own. So what was the use of her seeing that Hugh had plenty of vests and socks if the " greedy things " (meaning the brethren) were to take them away from him ? They were monks and greedy things, and Master Hugh would have to make his own bed, which he would never do properly, and empty his slops, which he would spill. So Hugh sent her a series of pictures portraying his arrival at Mirfield and the " greedy things " in cassocks running away in different directions with all his luggage. Other sketches showed him ringing a large dinner-bell to wake the greedy things in the morning, and upsetting his slop-pail.

Thus, not more than six months after we had settled in Winchester with such fair promise of content, it began to be clear that it was not answering. My mother still said nothing about her own view of the matter, as long as Winchester appeared to suit everybody else, but in her diary she wrote a few explicit words : " I sicken at all this everyday life, at the setting of it. Oh, the awful backwater this is! . . ." Just then I think she would have found every place in England a backwater ; even London, as the scene of her new and more restricted life, would not have been much better. But now Winchester was failing in other ways : the spring was raw and chilly, and the temporary improvement in Maggie's health and general spirits was arrested by increased physical discomfort and occasionally deep mental depression. She had not spent a winter in England for many years, and the mists and damp which hung in this hollow brought her barometer down to very unsettled weather. She was not in fit health to move about much, and she unerringly pointed out that the downs which afforded me such pleasant games of golf were seen by her through the dirty windows of a hired brougham ; " Put the windows down then " made her laugh, but it was really no laughing matter. She wanted change : everybody else hopped about while she moped on her perch : there was I, just going out to Athens again, and oh, the Acropolis. . . .

Hitherto she had accepted her disabilities with the gayest courage, making the uttermost of what her limitations left her, but now (and no wonder) her continued ill-health was at last wearing out the stoutness of her patience. If there was no more Athens and Egypt, could she not, at least, have the country, fields, animals, the green things, the live air? She had long and agitating talks with my mother, and then, while she bitterly blamed herself for complaining, she held on to the fact of her reasonableness. Each of them, one ill and depressed, the other unhappy and hopeless, was doing her very best, but those indefinable frictions which most strongly "rub up" those who love each other most, and which seem only to be aggravated by affection, made them both ache with a bewildered sense of estrangement.

It is hard to express another and more vital change that came over Maggie during this spring of 1898. She lost none of her essential sweetness of disposition, but there was added to it some sort of sternness, a new consciousness of responsibility. She was working at the proofs of a finished, though unpublished, manuscript of my father's on the Revelation of St. John, and it had got a great hold on her, not so much as a treatise in itself, but as a reflection of his mind; simultaneously she was in constant correspondence with my brother Arthur on the Life of my father which he was then writing. She was, in fact, as my mother subsequently noted, "soaking herself in him," and the effect of that appeared in her own bearing to her surroundings. She became markedly more like him in acts and attitudes, each small in itself, but like a painter's fine touches on his picture, bringing out an effect. These things were slight at first, like the unconscious imitative gestures made by someone who is strongly under the influence of another, and it was chiefly in her dealings with my mother that she exhibited them; if she thought she saw a slackness in domestic arrangements, she would, rather peremptorily, suggest a stricter policy. Insensibly she laid her hands on the reins, making the household to take its pace from her. And so eagerly did my mother accept such suggestions. . . . It was like *him* to want things done in that way; it was like her to be alert in such service again.

I went off to Athens soon after this stir and seething became apparent, with the impression that we should not be plums on the garden wall much longer. This expedition was no pleasure-excursion, but was undertaken in order to administer a fund initiated by the Duke of Westminster, and placed in the hands of the Red Cross for the relief of Greek refugees from Thessaly, which at the moment was in the hands of the victorious Turks at the close of the Græco-Turkish war. The Turkish armies, it may be remembered, had strolled across Thessaly with a minimum of opposition from the Greek troops, who, ill-organized, ill-supplied, ill-fed, and ill-led, had trotted away in front of them, until, when the southern boundaries of the province were reached, the powers which guaranteed the integrity of Greece bade the victors halt. The rout of the Greeks had been complete, and never had a war been so military-mild. The Greek army, to put it briefly, had got away from the advance of the Turkish line with the utmost possible expedition, and by one of those ironical happenings, which go far to support the existence of a humorous Providence, the first Greek soldier who arrived hot-foot in Athens was he who had won the Marathon race in the Olympic games two years before. So bravely and swiftly had he then run from Marathon to Athens that the experts marvelled at the speed of the man, saying that no known runner could normally go like that: the glory of winning the Marathon race must have been an inspiration to him, making him super-human in his prowess. Now he triumphantly vindicated his form: he was inspired to run like that again.

There was then an armistice, pending future arrangements, and the Turks observed it with the most scrupulous passivity. In the complete disintegration of any Greek fighting force, a mere handful of men was sufficient to hold the conquered province, and the embarkation of superfluous troops was in progress when I arrived at Volo. That day certain transports had been expected, which were delayed by a storm, and regiment after regiment of Turks had marched into the town to find that they must remain there instead of embarking. Streets and quays that night were paved with the houseless soldiers, while the Greek inhabitants of Volo continued to occupy their tranquil abodes. There was no eviction of these, or commandeering of their tenements; the victors lay out in the open and the vanquished slept in their beds. Never was there more perfect discipline, all night long no sound was heard but the tramp of sentries. The same men would, no doubt, have murdered every man and ravished every woman in the place, if there had not been an order, but they had been told to be quiet.

The province was swarming with brigands, almost entirely Greek, who had warily followed the march of the Turkish armies southward, and in their rear descended to get the gleanings in the villages of their own countrymen. I had been authorized in Athens to get a Greek guard, before going out into the country to distribute relief to the Greeks who were stranded there, but no such guard was obtainable, and, as I wanted to get on with my work, I went to Edhem Pasha, Commander-in-Chief of the Turkish army in Thessaly, to see if he would do anything for me. I explained the position : I was on an errand of succour to the Greeks, and he quite understood. Certainly I should have a Turkish guard to protect me from Greek bandits, whose countrymen I had come to aid. In the meantime, let us have dinner, and the guard would be ready in the morning. Edhem enjoyed, I think, this exhibition of cynical benevolence to his foes. After all, poor things, they had given very little trouble, and the civilians were in deadly plight, what with the necessary commandeering of provisions and the violent epidemic of small-pox, and he was very glad that something should be done for them. He described to me the famous battle of Pharsala, which had been hailed in Athens as a triumph of Greek arms. " That is surprising," he said, " for when we got into touch with the Greek army at Pharsala, all we had to do was to say ' Shoo, shoo,' and away they went. Our men call them the host of hares!" At parting, he gave me a set of Greek stamps with the Turkish surcharge, for use in Thessaly, while the province was in the hands of the Turks.

Next morning, accordingly, we started, and found a grim jetsam stranded in the towns and villages of the conquered province. All the inhabitants who had been able to secure any sort of conveyance had fled in front of the advancing Turks; there were left the poorest and those who from age or youth were most helpless. Food was scarce, the epidemic of small-pox was severe, and the Greek doctor whom we had brought from Athens soon had his hands full. He made the best of the filthy and verminous conditions for those who were down with it, and with a gay and guileful tongue (as in some story by Kipling) he induced the rest to submit to vaccination, which they regarded as a perilous adventure not unconnected with black arts. Various were his blandishments and menaces: to one it was the King who had ordered that all who would not be vaccinated should be clapped into gaol: to another it was Queen Victoria who had sent the vaccine: to an aged crone it was that vaccine was an elixir, which would make her so lovely that all the young men of Larissa would sigh their hearts out for her.

Then there were destitute folk to be taken to refuge camps round Athens, and soup-kitchens to be organized, and Lady Egerton, wife of the British Minister, set on foot admirable institutions where women who could weave were given employment. A couple of months' work relieved the worst distress and brought us to the end of our funds, and, after a week or two more in Athens, I turned homewards, stopping on the way with a friend who had a house on the island of Capri. When I got home I was told by Lord Wantage, the head of the Red Cross, that King George of Greece had expressed an amiable desire to decorate with the Order of the Redeemer two of those who had been engaged in this relief work, and that my name had been recommended. But from that day to this I never heard a word more about it, and the mystery as to whether the Order of the Redeemer was lost in the post, or whether King George, on second thoughts, considered that it would be too much pleasure, remains unsolved.

But on that idle visit to Capri a spell wove itself, and it became to me the Enchanted Island. It was not the first or the second time that I had been there, but hitherto no magic had stirred there : it had been but a place of pleasant vineyards and cobbled paths, of warm still nights, of mornings of pellucid swimmings, and afternoons of walks to breezy uplands, and returns in mellow dusks. Certainly it had been charming, but with an external charm only. Now, as by a wand invisibly waved and by mutterings of incantation, the spell was made, and I found myself no longer a vagrant traveller, but a home-sick and returning wanderer. Capri, hitherto lovely but aloof, had without warning made a breach in my heart, and through it triumphantly tumbled Italy itself. The fact of Italy got inside me; never since have I gone there without the sense of homing.

How exquisite is this multiplication of homes which fetter the heart and thereby enlarge its freedom! I should like to be at home in a hundred countries, feeling that I was knit to them by some psychical bond as much thicker than blood as blood is thicker than water. The merely travelled cosmopolitan may feel at ease in many countries and with many tongues, and yet be no more than a courier in Babel, but the cosmopolitanism of the heart transforms the well-equipped traveller into a native; he lies a-soak instead of sight-seeing. There were the same lizards (or, if not, their descendants: I do not know the length of a lizard's life), and certainly the same stone walls and sea and olive-trees, the same houses and vineyards, and the same inhabitants; the same footfalls and snatches of songs and whistlings that drifted in the dusk by the Villa Ferraro up and down the cobbled ways, but now the singing was within me, and the footfalls echoed in my heart. The spell did not arise from any mental perception, from a comprehension of the Italian or Caprese point of view: it was rather that by some magic of the whitest they had grasped me. Was it some baptism of water that I had unwittingly undergone in flashing noondays at the Bagno Timberino, where the gigantic ruins of the imperial palace have tumbled from the cliff, and the water of the tideless sea eternally strives to wash the antique wickedness from them? or was it some baptism of fire, some sacrament of the sun which I had received, or of glowing cigarette-ends smoked beneath the stars, or of Naples smouldering on the horizon, or of the glow of the burning which is never quenched illuminating the wreathed vapours about Vesuvius?

Since then Capri has never ceased to hold some postern in my heart, at the door of which, when I enter, I sprinkle myself with the holy water of

Lethe, and at that lustral touch all memories of duties omitted and deeds committed lose coherence and significance, and become, at the most, a misty food for Freud. It was only with an effort that I could realize that I had been among stricken refugees in Thessaly : so long ago and so far away it was, that probably it did not happen to me at all, but to some previous incarnation of me, incredibly remote. Even Naples across the bay was only a streak of light, to be regarded as one regards through a telescope the star-dust of the heavens, and wonders, with a sense of fairy-tale, whether, indeed, those luminous atoms are worlds which have their own inhabitants. All that matters is that one is dropping down the path which lies between the olive-groves on one hand and the sunk vineyards on the other, and that at the next corner the bay of bathing will come into sight, and that for three hours there will be liquid pilgrimages of coolness and baskings on the beach that quivers with the stir of heat. Then there will be food and wine, and after wine the winking of eyelids and their closing, and the waking to the rustle of the sea-breeze, and a climb up Monte Solaro, where the tawny lilies lurk in the grass. Soon the sunset will fade and the stars steal from their celestial lairs, and when picquet and the piano are done, a crawl to bed, and a waking to another day precisely like the last. And over all, a balm and an anæsthetic to any restless piece of conscience, lies the sense of being very busy. That is Capri's crowning conjuring-trick: the conviction that the day has been well and strenuously spent hovers like a benediction by your bedside. " Sleep, weary one," it whispers. " Get a good rest : your ardent spirit deserves eight hours of profound slumber. Remember you have a heavy day in front of you, what with bathing and siesta. . . ."

I clung to each day as my departure grew imminent, as to the last hours of a holiday which must be squeezed of the last drop of juice, till the moment when I should see the white wake of water behind the crazy little steamer that was bearing me back to Naples grow longer and ever longer, and the figures on the quay fade to indistinguishable specks : for I knew from letters I had received that there were difficulties and decisions ahead in the hyperborean island. When I got home they were still a little vague, matters for hint not statement, but they quickly became definite.

" Throughout May and June "—such was the upshot of talks with my mother—" it was piping hot here, and stuffy. We all felt it rather, and

Maggie was laid flat, and, oh, my dear, how lovely Capri must have been for them as likes being broiled, and Athens too, though your account of the small-pox made me squirm. Yes, Maggie! She has been trying so hard, bless her, but she has had a time of dreadful depression, partly physical, no doubt, partly the heat. . . ."

And the dear face grew troubled, and piece by piece, with self-blame for not being wiser, and for being a Selfish Pig, all the tangle and the uncertainty and some deep-lying, hardly acknowledged uneasiness emerged. Maggie had been suffering from just such depressions as my father was subject to (here was another point of resemblance in that curious change which was taking place in her), and now, just as in the old years, they had produced in my mother some fettered sense of bondage. She had never, when they were upon him, been able to proceed normally and light-heartedly with life (which would probably have been the best thing to do), for fear that, in all innocence, she might be displeasing him and vexing him. These darknesses had been like an obsession to him, and he was in bondage, too, till they lifted. And now the same sort of visitation had come to Maggie, and what was to be done, and to what did it point? Hitherto Maggie had taken her ailments with such pluck and defiance, refusing to let them touch her essentially, but holding them at arm's length, as external disturbances. And as for the pitched tent in Winchester, it was horribly dull for Maggie here: she could not for ever poke and prowl in this little walled-in garden: she wanted, as with thirst, a greater spaciousness, and, in her inability to walk much, something to manage strollingly, pigeons and poultry and flower beds. There was no such diversion for her here; when she had read and written to weariness, there was nothing that refreshed while it occupied her. Never did advocate speak so convincingly for a cause that enlisted her own personal sympathy, and yet at that time there was no one to whom personally country-life appealed less.

She saw another thing, too, in her wisdom. Strangely and somewhat disconcertingly there was developing in Maggie the trait so characteristic of my father, the love of organizing, the shouldering of responsibilities. In our mixed natures (for no man is wholly a man, nor any woman entirely feminine) some masculine fibre had begun to assert itself in her.

" In the country she can have her sphere," said

my mother. "Something to look after. A sphere."

She loved a catch-word like that: an idea always became more definite and a difficulty more soluble when she had affixed its label.

And so, by degrees, the fact that we must fold our tents like the Arabs—as if we had not had enough of Egypt already!—and silently steal away, began to ooze into the water-supply of domestic life, somehow hardening it, and producing reticences and changes of subject. Orders to view houses arrived, and casual airy references to Basingstoke and Haslemere developed into visits of inspection, and there we all were, my mother regarding the prospect of exclusive country-life with sheer blank dismay; Maggie silent and depressed; I, so much disliking the idea of leaving Winchester that I could take only the most frigid interest in these "orders to view," and all of us unsettled at the thought of another move, and shrinking from discussion. But clearly Winchester would not do, and the knowledge of that was somehow like a street band playing at a distance: it did not interrupt, but slightly embarrassed, conversation. Only if a silence fell, the band became more audible: it was certainly moving up in our direction, and would come to the front door before long. There it would stay until the organ, and the billiard-table, and the statue of Rameses the Great, and the folio editions of the Christian Fathers, were all vomited out of No. 9, St. Thomas's Street again, and were taken away to Basingstoke or Haslemere or wherever.

What we all wanted was what in clerical language is termed " a call." We were a most united family, reinforced by a devoted and beloved friend of my mother's, and we depended on each other and were fond of each other to a degree rather unusual among a family of adults, so that if it had been needful for the work of one of us or the health of another to go to a definite place, we should have played hymns of festival on the organ till the very moment when the packers seized it. But there was no such call, except the call to be gone from Winchester, and that was only a negative one, not, in fact, a call of " Come here," but only " Go away." That autumn in consequence was, from a purely material point of view, the climax of the effect of my father's death. Before, we had to be at Lambeth or Addington if we wanted to be at home, and there were no two words to be said about it. We were attached to the full orb of his office, and rolled along the sky as his fixed satellites. But now we were all

MOTHER

adrift, and individual preferences came in, and there was no reason to be in any one place rather than any other, provided only that it was not a provincial town in a cup-shaped hollow.

I had begun to think that there would be a long respite before any further move, for the house at Haslemere wouldn't do, and the house near Basingstoke was an abomination, when there was detected, in the fell pages of *Country Life*, an advertisement with an odiously attractive illustration of a house with manageable acreage, and an avenue of pines, standing on high sandy soil within forty miles of London. It was of red brick, chiefly Jacobean, and seemed a terribly amiable dwelling. But there was the brief consolation of hoping that it was all too good to be true, and it seemed most unlikely that there should, either in Sussex or anywhere else, be a place called Horsted-Keynes. It was the kind of name that a foreign author writing about rural England would invent.

But there was a Horsted-Keynes: trains went there, and Lucy went in one of them, and when she returned she was like the Queen of Sheba when she beheld the glory of Solomon, except that instead of having no spirit left in her, she had a great deal. *Country Life*, apparently, had not told the half of the charm and beauty of Tremans. And thus, for the last time, my mother moved her earthly habitation, and lived at Tremans longer than she had lived in any of her previous homes.

CHAPTER IV

A ROAD sunk deep between hedges and sandy banks slopes downwards from the village of Horsted-Keynes, and passes on the right a gate leading into a short avenue of big pines which grow out of a clipped yew hedge, over the top of which you can see various and fantastic chimneys of red-brick, a small lead-cowled turret, and the gables of tiled roofs. A hundred yards within the gate the pines cease, and the road takes a sharp-angled turn below a great walnut-tree. The house then faces you across a lawn, enclosed by a low red-brick wall with a gate in the centre. Here was the original main entrance to the house, as the big door set on three curved stone steps testifies, but to-day you must proceed farther round a little wing of Elizabethan building to arrive at the more convenient access, which lies in an angle between this Elizabethan portion and a further small wing of grey stone with mullioned windows. A garden of flowers and espaliered fruit-trees and vegetables, grass-pathed, and sheltered on the north by a high wall and on the east by an immense yew hedge, lies to the right, and below it an orchard of apples and tall pink-flowering cherry-trees. Still moving round the house you come to a terraced bowling-green bounded by more yew hedges and the avenue of pines under which you have lately passed, and the lawn across which you first faced the house completes the circuit. Below, half hidden behind a row of unpruned shrubs and a herbaceous border, rise the lichened roofs of barns and farm-buildings, and the ground slopes gently down across hay-fields to a brook that prowls along the bottom of the valley, among fine oaks and an undergrowth of holly and hazel, and, making a juncture with two other streams, saunters into the Ouse and so past Lewes to the sea.

I cannot disentangle from the overlying memories of change and efflorescence a certain bareness in the garden when first I saw it. But when last I saw it in 1919, it was difficult to imagine a fairer place, so sweetly it rioted with the scent and colour of homely blossoms. The bowling-green, long grown tussocky and uneven, could not have been reclaimed without complete relaying, and since there was no clamour to play bowls, it was given a more decorative mission. Young apple-trees were planted there and thousands of bulbs, a milky way of the stars of spring. Jonquil and narcissus were there, and speckled fritillaries, and tulips, white-chaliced and red and yellow, and above all there were daffodils, daffodils so innumerable that when one day, owing to an undesired wealth of dandelions, I secretly picked every single dandelion-head that was in flower, and brought my family to see the Sisyphus-labour that I had accomplished, they could none of them discern any diminution of gold, and I had to tell them what I had done. So much for daffodils.

There, too, on the banks of the bowling-green were bushes of rosemary and broom and peonies, and round two sides of it a hedge of crimson rambler-rose, and the new sappy stems of each year were trained back into it, so that the hedge should not grow too high and hide the daffodils, but should become thick and very rosey. Below the bowling-green, round the small lawn that faced the house, there were flower-beds, and those just below the windows were always, at their season, tawny with wall-flowers, and their fragrance, redolent of unrecapturable memories and the dim early brightnesses of life, wandered in at the windows. Later in the year begonias made a stricter formality, and later yet dahlias and scarlet salvias. Round the other sides of the lawn there were beds that were always sanctuaries for blueness, of delphiniums and cornflowers, and nemesia and gentian and forget-me-not, and over the stone pilasters and balls of the gateway towards the walnut-tree pink rambler and purple clematis fought out a championship for twenty year-long rounds, and at the end both antagonists were still going strong.

A pergola of small white climbing rose darkened the path that led round the angle of the house between the bowling-green and the garden of mixed flowers and fruit. A wall sheltered that acre from the north wind, but whatever wind it was that blew, the spices of it flowed forth. Under its protection was a tiled space that caught the sun from morning till the shadow of the house lay across it, and lemon verbena flanked it and aromatic geranium: it was a "smellage" of fragrant plants, and in front was a trellis of sweet-briar, through which in due season came the scent of the bean flower, and the sun cooked a grill of manifold deliciousness, and the breeze stirred it. Pear-trees were spread on the wall, and a morning-glory testified with uncurled trumpets to the night dew. At the end of this garden rose the smooth green serge of that astounding yew hedge, and against it burned the yellow flame of broom and the smoulder of Oriental poppies. Green woodpeckers nested in the orchard below, and great-tits behind a displaced stone in the wall close at hand: they had chosen their nursery cunningly, but gave their secret away by loud scoldings when you approached it. And owls, owls! Tremans will always be to me the place of owls; the barn owl was always whitely hunting over the bowling-green in a silence broken by those shrieks so disconcerting to those who do not love it, and, when its dinner was done, snoring in the ivy, and the tawny owl was there more elusive and mysterious, emending his Shakespeare and calling, "Hoo-hoo, whoo-it, whoo, hoo," and the little owl was there, the wicked little owl, mewing according to his wickedness.

Embowered thus stood the serene old house, low-ceilinged, with panelled parlours, and broad oak staircases and spacious lobbies. Girt with the green freshness of its lawns, it was cool always in any stress of summer, and in the winter it had its open fireplaces, each with its bellows for the brisker burning of the logs, and (be it whispered) central heating to reinforce their flames. Of ancient oak was its woodwork, panels and floors and staircases, so seasoned that never a creak or a crack betrayed an insolidity, and here and there in third-story rooms and passages the beams of its construction were grey between the spaces of lath and plaster. It was always faintly fragrant with the smell of wood smoke (for in winter the fires never died down on the hearths), even when through the windows in summer there flowed the scent of wall-flowers, or when the lilacs were in bloom. But something more fragrant yet was to be fashioned there, and I think that if the house stood for another thousand years, there would never fade from the cool dusk of its rooms and passages, or from its sunny garden, the aroma of the years when my mother was the lamp and the light of it, and its ruins would be haunted and blessed by her still. . . .

So the stream of vomiting vans which brought Winchester to Tremans, poured down the avenue of pines, and unladed themselves below the wisteria that in this hot April was heavy with bunches of blossom. Out came Rameses and the organ and the early Christian Fathers, and with a sunken heart I dustily saw to their new bestowal. Once again Taffy lay in the mid-stream of traffic, and the Persian cat smelt familiar objects and saw that they were put in places that were satisfactory to her Oriental Highness, and once again Matilda was convinced with the granite imperturbability of her Druidical mind that all that was being done for her special amusement. She had learned everything that was to be known about life and death and house-moving, and this pilgrimage from Winchester (so I read Matilda's mind) was to her no more than the film or moving picture of a quite familiar scene. Then, even in the midst of this vain-glorious thought, Matilda's world-weary ear caught a new noise coming in through the open window, by which her cage was set. She had never heard such a sound at Lambeth (Matilda used not to go to Addington), nor had it ever penetrated into her apartments at St. Thomas's Street, Winchester, but now its reiteration proved that it was no fantasy of her own imaginative brain. It said " Cuckoo, cuckoo," and Matilda thought about it in dead silence for three days, and paid no more attention to our pushings and pullings, but retired into some remote shrine of abstract meditation. The choicest pieces of banana fell from her claws, her ear was deaf to the groan of creaking furniture and the crash of broken crockery, for she knew all about that. Then she came out of her retreat, cleared her throat like the kitchen-maid, and said "Cuckoo, cuckoo, cuckoo" for a week.

But what was I to do when the organ was in place again and the folios of the early Christian Fathers were on the shelves ? I had not learned the wisdom of Matilda, nor had I Matilda's genius thus to be able to brood and ponder, self-involved and contemplative, and be calmly content on re-emergence with having reproduced exactly what I meant to reproduce. I had my own work to amuse and absorb me, but both during it, and in the longer intervals when one story was done and another not yet begun, I wanted two things, relaxation and stimulus, not, be it understood, in the bullion of love and affection which would gleam here inexhaustibly, but in small change, in change, indeed, so small that the very mention of its coinage sounds ridiculous.

But there it was : I wanted golf and games and ease and casual intercourse with those of my own sex. Just as a woman, if she has any semblance of intellectual life of her own, demands, though blissfully married, some sort of female companionship, so, too, a man, especially if he is not married, and lives a good deal among the conundrums and portrayals and pictures which he conjures up

MOTHER

in his own mind, and (rightly or wrongly) strives to commit to paper, needs most imperatively some commerce with his own sex. His enjoyment of it may to an external view only express itself in grunts and grumblings, in putting his feet upon a chair and yawning, but it is as necessary for him as for the body is necessary the supply of some obscure vegetable salt. It gives nutriment, perhaps, to some ductless gland in which is involved the due and orderly function of his physical economy. Not every day or all day does a man want one of his own sex to be accessible, but I doubt whether a young man can sustain any sort of part in a permanent home, remotely situated in the country, of which the household entirely consists of women, unless he has some sort of male companionship.

In that divine month of May which followed, these conclusions became dimly apparent. The daily problem of what to do after lunch, for instance, grew insoluble. The morning could be busily occupied, but could Priapus himself have been content with the garden every afternoon, or anyone but Mr. Wordsworth have been content to " wander lonely as a cloud " through these delightful vales and uplands, and perpetually fill his heart with pleasure and dance with the daffodils? After lunch a melancholy quiet submerged the house, for all the others " rested," and I felt, with Œnone, that " I alone awake." Seven miles on a bicycle, it is true, would bring me to the golf-links on Ashdown Forest, but would you, though you were quite devoted to golf, constantly struggle uphill for four miles and downhill for three, in order to play a round, and, returning, wheel your bicycle uphill for three miles, and pedal easily along for four? Or could you play croquet eagerly and angrily with someone who did not really care whether she won or not? Games of every sort must be deadly serious, if they are to be played at all, and no member of my family, except Hugh, ever understood this. But the real lack at Tremans as a permanent home was the absence of a male with whom at ease one could discuss and quarrel and conspire. . . . With what wistfulness, day by day, did my mother ask me what I was going to do that afternoon! I had no idea.

It was not that I was idle: for I was deeply immersed in a sensational tale called *The Luck of the Vails*. The germ of it was a story that Arthur had told his boys at Eton: this he presented to me with the rhyming legend which ran

round the rim of the jewelled cup which was the
"Luck" and the clue of the tale:

> "When the Luck of the Vails is lost,
> Fear not rain nor fire nor frost;
> When the Luck is found again,
> Fear both fire and frost and rain."

That uncanny and suggestive rhyme fermented in my brain with yeasty bubblings, and I enjoyed for months the heavenly illusion which comes sometimes to scribblers that their puppets and the adventures of them have an existence more real than that of the folk among whom they live. The great yew hedge in my tale became the *real* yew hedge, and the hedge at Tremans from which I took it was but shadowy in comparison. . . .

One night, during the writing of it, I vividly remember as spiced with a pungent and pleasing horror. I was quite alone in the house on that February evening, for the rest of the family were up in London, and there was a gale bugling outside which caused the curtains in the drawing-room, where I worked after a lonely dinner, eerily to stir and rustle, and their fringes whispered over the floor as they mysteriously bellied and grew lean again. The wind hooted in the open chimney, making the blazing logs flare high and die down again, and, as I followed the villain of the tale, who had quite taken charge of me, through the maze of his infamies, there came little tappings on the dark panels from the pictures that stirred in the draught, and more than once I had to cast a terrified glance round the dim room, to be sure that no stranger presence had slid in. Then a servant came in with a tray of spirits and siphon, and I heard her steps die away.

There was then a wicked uncle, Uncle Francis, in that obsolete story of mine, and he was frightening me. I knew what he was meaning to do, for I had invented it myself, but the writing of it down vitalized him into something real and external, and he was horribly present. I wanted to stop working, but apart from the fact that I was completely unable to do so, I was wise enough to know that it was a shocking waste not to use such a mood as I was in, to the utmost final flicker of it. On the other hand, if Uncle Francis was to get much more dreadful, I should not in the least enjoy putting out the lights, and going up to bed with a candle that wagged in the air-currents and cast disconcerting shadows on the walls. So, very prudently, I resolved to get safely to my bedroom, shut the door, and have no post-midnight excursion through the very staircase and landing, 'on which, in my fiction, Uncle Francis was busy with his "negotium in tenebris." So with my pen in my mouth (and my heart there too), and my manuscript and my cigarettes, I went to my room, prepared for a harrowing vigil. I must confess that when I got there I looked in a large wardrobe to guard against surprises, and examined the alcoves of the windows over which the curtains were drawn.

Uncle Francis (to my mind) was in admirable form, and I quaked as I wrote. And then suddenly the most awful thing happened. I was meditating the end of a sentence with my eyes just a little raised from my paper, when I saw a lighted candle move in front of me, and then another, and the dark semblance of the figure of a man was seated between them. . . . I sprang to my feet with a catch in my breath, to find that the door of the wardrobe, which had a long looking-glass let into it, had swung noiselessly open, suddenly confronting me with the reflection of myself and my candles. . . .

In this picture of early days at Tremans I have laid on all my own shadows first and left the prevailing sunlight to the end. That shone with a brilliance beyond all expectation, and for the next six years Maggie's life blossomed with activity and happiness. Delicate she would always be, but once again that invincible mind of hers, which had barely dragged itself along under the weight of infirmities and depressions at Winchester, shook off the dust and soared. This keen, kind air, which in the heat was bracing, and brisk in the cold, was exactly what her body needed, and with no less exactitude had my mother forecast the value of a " sphere " for her. That late-born instinct, almost reincarnating in her my father's spirit, was just as dominant as it had been when first it awoke in her, but now it had its sphere to dominate, instead of stifling and struggling in the mire of ill-health. Everything out of doors in farm and garden was included in that sphere: more flower-beds must be mapped, more yews must be planted. A sundial: it was an anachronism not to have a sundial, and the standard of it must be voluted—give me a bit of paper—thus, to reproduce that twisted chimney. The great granite head of Pasht must stand somewhere near: his centuries of sculptured repose would be a counterblast to the shifting shadow, in case we were inclined to think time too short, and hurry to conclusions. Then the whole of the bowling-green must be planted with bulbs, not a clump here and a clump there, as in the foolish London parks, but with something of the free irregularity of stars in the summer night.

MOTHER

"I'm afraid I should have put the stars in patterns," said she, "if I had been asked to arrange them, and it would have been a great mistake. And bulbs——"

"It would have been rather pretty," said somebody.

"Yes: rather pretty, and how tired you would have got of it. It's the same with bulbs. The right way—yes, I know—the right way will be to take handfuls of bulbs, throw them into the air, and plant them where they come down."

She hastily turned over the leaves of a gardening-book. "The way to plant bulbs is this," she said. "You dig a hole four feet deep for each bulb——"

"Too shallow," said somebody, with withering sarcasm.

"I mean four inches deep—I said four inches—and before you put the bulb in, sprinkle some sand in the hole. Oh, there's the cart come back from the station. That's brought the wire-netting for the hen-run. I must just go and see if it *is* it. Nettie" (to a friend), "if you haven't anything particular to do this minute, you might just start them laying the bricks for the column for the head of Pasht. Two feet each way."

"You told me to read the proofs of your second

chapter on the excavations," said Nettie, after thought.

"Maggie dear, hadn't you better go and rest?" said my mother. "Dr. Todd told you to rest for half an hour before lunch."

"But he didn't know the wire for the hen-run was coming to-day. I will rest longer after lunch: I will really. Oh, bother, there's Beth with my medicine."

"Nay now, don't say bother!" said Beth.

"I shall. Do you remember when we were little, how you used to pretend to taste our medicine, and smack your lips and say, ' Oh, how good ! ' "

"Well, then, if it made you swallow it up," said Beth. "And I'm sure you've all done enough work for to-day."

Then Taffy's education must be seen to, and a revolving summer-house for the orchard which could be turned to catch or avoid the sun, and entrap a breeze or exclude a wind. Its ugly corrugated roof must be thatched, and some roots of heather anchored there to see if they would grow (they did), and a dovecote must be erected hard by, for the cooing promoted meditation, and a pea-hen must be found for the bachelor peacock with the crumpled foot, who used to run behind the victoria in order to admire his reflection in the japanned panel at the back. He ran, gazing at himself, as far as the gate into the pine-avenue, so fascinated by the contemplation of his own beauty that when the carriage slowed down to take the corner, he hit his beak against the adorable image of himself. But he behaved kindly to the white pea-hen, which was somehow procured (alive) at Leadenhall market, though in her milk-white bosom there beat a black heart. For when, in the following spring, she laid a quantity of eggs, she neglected her maternal duty of keeping them warm, and gadded about. The eggs, consequently, became addled, as anyone could tell who went near the cold nest, and then, too late, her conscience pricked her, and she incubated, in that stench, day and night to the detriment of her health. So in all kindness the eggs were taken away and buried as deep as Maggie wanted to plant the bulbs, and finding the nest empty, the white pea-hen saw red, and with hoarse cries rushed down to the chicken-yard, and killed four hens. She had to be got rid of after that, and Maggie sold her, without a character, at a staggering loss.

It was not only in the masterly management

(apart from pea-hens) of all these rural vocations that Maggie's convalescence manifested itself. She organized and started, quite with my father's impulsive enthusiasm, which made those under him devote themselves to his schemes, a society called the St. Paul's Association for Biblical Study. It met monthly in London, for the purpose of hearing an address (followed by discussion) from some eminent theologian, and presently Maggie started, on the same lines, another society that held its meetings in the Long Vacation at Oxford or Cambridge. Not only was her finger on the pulses of these, it was more her blood which made their pulses to beat, for she kept them nourished and vigorous. Now, too, before we had been a year at Tremans, there was also a *pied-à-terre* in London, for Lucy had taken a tiny house in Barton Street, Westminster, had added on to it, and it was a minute caravanserai to which all of us were welcome up to the limits of its accommodation, and Maggie often stayed there for those full and busy days of which now she was capable again. Her whole life was a-bloom with its final flowering.

This resurgence of vitality in my sister, after the years of invalid life, during which my mother had watched over her and protected her from all that overtaxed the small store of strength with which she had to combat illness, necessitated a definite change of relationship between them. Hitherto the management of the entire family life had been on my mother's shoulders: it was she who had oiled the wheels, and held the reins, and blown the horn, and driven the coach; she had been ostler and guard and coachman in one. But now, with Maggie's accession of strength, and in particular with the growing psychical resemblance between her and my father, the rôles were to some extent reversed. The male element, the desire for a "sphere," which my mother had so clearly foreseen and so warmly welcomed, required readjustments to be made, and these involved a profound and delicate point of psychology. Those instincts for responsibility and management in Maggie did not in any way supplant her feminine tenderness or dependence on my mother, the two existed in her, separately and distinctly, but as allies and not antagonists. Eagerly had my mother leaped to welcome the new development, beholding, with a pang of wonder and love, that Maggie had passed through a new birth. She had come forth after that long trance of illness with a changed nature, her father's. But the old mind was there as well, subtly mingled with the new, so that while Maggie took the reins, and managed and assumed responsibilities, she was still wanting to sit inside the coach with the windows adjusted to her liking, and the cushions ready, and herself protected and sheltered. There was my mother, anxious to fit herself into Maggie's attitude, but how was that possible? She demanded things incompatible, for however well you can both swim and fly, you cannot perform both motions simultaneously. There were debates and misunderstandings and explanations, for there were engaged two extremely analytical minds, which had to pierce to the core of the matter. What made the poignancy of the situation was that between them there existed an undying love, which at the end, after the storm and the darkness which were coming, shone out again in luminous serenity.

My own situation, however, in that delicious house, showed no sign of amelioration, but grew steadily worse. I was already thirty-two, an age at which most young men have gone out into the world on an independent footing of their own, with, in the majority of cases, the tie of marriage, and this shallow life, unnaturally devoid of any initiative or ordinary companionships, grew impossible. I might with reasonable geniality have made a much better job of it than I did, but I doubt whether any one with real activity of mind and body could have made a good job of it, unless he had been a country-lover of the very highest grade. Probably it was a mistake to have tried this experiment of living at Tremans at all, when the prescience of failure had been so strong, and the only excuse to be made for the error was that I had a very genuine desire to fulfil the promise I had made at my father's death to live with my mother.

But now it became clear to her and to me that the promise could not be kept in such an environment as she had chosen, for out of her anxiety and my depression there was coming between us a barrier of some kind, a sense of isolation and estrangement which was utterly intolerable. For that I was quite to blame, for I had never really torn up the indictment against them all that they had gone to Tremans knowing how I disliked it, and then were disappointed and sad because I did not enjoy it. It was that which I used as an excuse, if not a justification, for my own disagreeableness and despair: I kept telling myself that it was their fault. . . . And in her wisdom and her sweetness all those abominable months, she watched and sorrowed and forgave, and after a year of it, she saw that this was no good at all, and it must be stopped. She did not put her pride in her pocket, for she had no pride, and her pocket was full of love which would not see itself shadowed or dimmed, and while I was away on some visit, she wrote me the perfect pearl of a letter. She said that she had been afraid, before we came to Tremans, that I should find it an impossible life; it was that which made her of so divided a heart when the decision was taken. Since then she had seen that it was so, and we must not let it go on like this. . . . She remembered my promise, and she thanked and loved me for it, and now she wished to set me free from it. . . . And so her house ceased in one sense to be mine for the first time in my life, and I settled into a small flat in Oxford Street. And in another sense Tremans became much more "home" than in all the days of my sojourn there.

Then I intensely disliked it, but now, not being rooted there, I began to love it, and all its sweet ways, with an ever-growing affection. That sounds, as Beth said when she heard I was going away, "contrary enough" ("Eh, don't leave us," she said. "Pray-a-don't be so contrary"). But it was not so contrary as it sounded, for thus the division between my mother and myself was broken like match-wood. . . .

CHAPTER V

BAIREUTH, as it was when first I saw it, in the summer of 1899, was like some stupendous comet once for a series of years coming brilliantly close to the earth, and then never appearing again. It has vanished utterly, not a gleam of its true glory is left in the heavens, and as those who saw it at its brightest are few and will soon be fewer, I propose to recall it in an immense parenthesis. . . .

In that year, Baireuth had climbed to the zenith of its brilliance in the heavens of music. Before the next festival, two years after, when I was at Baireuth again, it was a receding comet, and its brightness was waning. Now it blazed; it was Mecca set on the summit of Parnassus, and from the musical world of all countries the adoring pilgrims flocked to the shrine. Wagner opera was supreme: the Wagnerites out-shouted everybody else, and chanted, with the solemn sanctity of a creed, the dogma that the Master was the supreme and final incarnation of the spirit of music (for there had been no true incarnation before, neither could such come after), and that the supreme expression of music was, with the single exception of the Siegfried Idyll, opera. The second clause in the creed, after the definition of the Master, was that at Baireuth only, and nowhere else, was it possible to be witness of his glory. The *Festspiel* at Baireuth was the only true revelation: all others were heretical. The third clause ordained that you had to leave the critical spirit behind you when you came to Baireuth, in order that you might be in a fit state to receive the initiation. Just at this epoch, then, Baireuth was at its zenith, and even at the next festival, a certain *Dämmerung* had fallen on this Mecca of music: it no longer basked in exclusive effulgence. Already Munich had instituted a festival, which immediately followed on that of Baireuth, and at Munich were performed (with the exception of *Parsifal*) such works of the Master as had not been given there. Thus, if your cycle at Baireuth had consisted of the *Ring* and the *Meistersinger*, with a *Parsifal* at each end, you would hear at Munich *Tristan* and *Tannhäuser* and the rest, and apostates began to whisper, under risk of the rack, that really, you know, Munich in some ways was quite up to—and the faithful looked pained and pitiful, and skilfully changed the subject. . . . Then at Munich you could hear Mozart as well, and the faithful smiled indulgently, and kindly said that they had always been told that *Figaro* was very pretty.

Then the dusk grew denser, for Hans Richter, the great prop and pillar of Baireuth, the initiated priest (for had he not received consecration at the Master's hands in the matter of conducting *Parsifal* and the other gospels?), accepted a post at Manchester, and degraded his inspired baton with performances at Covent Garden. At that, out of the darkening and thunderous glow, a flash of lightning smote him, for Frau Cosima Wagner, widow and priestess of the Master, caused him to be described in the programme of the approaching festival, as Hans Richter of Manchester. Why he did not instantly expire at the stroke of this ironical thunderbolt was never clearly known, but he certainly survived it, and was not even paralysed, and conducted at Covent Garden quite efficiently. Indeed, his apostasy expanded into further blasphemies, for in my own hearing he said that Wagner-opera would one day *return* to Germany, not squawled or shrieked, but sung, and that it would return from England. As Jean and Edouard de Reszke, and Plançon and Ternina, were doing their best about that time to sing it in

London, there was something to be said for his heresy. But he paid dearly, that supreme musician, for his friendship and faithfulness to England, for, after the declaration of war, stories, coming from Germany, were circulated about him to the effect that he had given the English medals which he had received, to be melted down into bullion for the Fatherland. Though widely believed here, there was no word of truth in it: Hans Richter never did anything of the sort. But it was a thoroughly Teutonic reprisal for his belief in England, to discredit him with the English.

The two final and extinguishing darknesses that befell Baireuth, more dense than any yet, were the expiration of the copyright of *Parsifal*, which hitherto could only be given there, and the outbreak of the European War. After these, it can never recover the sacred and sacramental supremacy which it enjoyed before, nor ever again shall we see, there or elsewhere, that crowd of devout worshippers hurrying into the dim, huge theatre, when the horns gave out from the roof the leading motif of the next act, with such expectancy of rapture and initiation as their cosmopolitan countenances then expressed. So, as that epoch is dead and will have no resurrection, it is allowable to attempt to indicate the incredible atmosphere, subtly induced, which encompassed it.

Baireuth itself is a mean and ugly little Bavarian town, dull and smelly and sultry. There is nothing whatever of beauty to recommend it, and apart from some barrack-like sort of palace, the creation of King Ludwig, the only notable building there is the opera-house, acoustically admirable, but otherwise an abominaton of hideousness, which stands a mile or so out of the sleepy, bourgeois town, on a fringe of pinewoods. But during the festival, Baireuth had its court and its queen, all the more majestic for being uncrowned, and she, of course, was Frau Cosima Wagner, widow of the Master, and she was surrounded by the princes and princesses of her marriages. I went out this year with Mary, Countess of Galloway, who was a bosom friend of the family, and thus, rather reluctantly, I saw, as from the vestry of the cathedral, the robing and decoration of the priests and ministers who celebrated the Wagner-mass. There were several daughters, called after the heroines of the gospels, Eva and Elsa and Isolde, and one son, Siegfried, whose appearance and musical talents made one somehow think of his father's: there was a family resemblance, they were cast in the immortal mould. He and his sister Isolde were children of the Master; one of the other daughters (or was it both of them?) was the child of von Bülow, Frau Cosima's first husband, whom she left, at the Master's wish (and no doubt her own), to become the Master's wife. His genius demanded her, and her obedient husband acquiesced. She became Frau Cosima Wagner, for Wagner, already married, had got rid of his first wife. Then there were a couple of sons-in-law, and these comprised the royal family, and lived as in a royal palace, at Villa Wahnfried.

Far and away the most remarkable of them all, she, in fact, by whose inspiration and untiring energy Baireuth had become the sacred and central Mecca in the world of music, was Frau Cosima. *Parsifal*, I think, had only been performed at one festival during the Master's lifetime: *Tannhäuser* had been booed from the boards in Paris; his music was regarded in England, even after his visit there and the concert he conducted in the Albert Hall, as something decadent and maniacal, and the *culte*, though enthusiastically supported in Germany, was, at Wagner's death, only in its infancy. Without

Frau Cosima it could never, in so short a period, have attained to its cosmopolitan supremacy. She had an inexorable will, a dynamic power of " drive," of filling her workers and ministers with the enthusiasm of her own faith, and just now she was poised on the very attainment and apex of her life-long mission to convert the whole world to orthodox worship at the Holy City. There was no limit to her devotion, her absolutism, and her orthodoxy. One festival would hardly be over before she began working for the next, and I well remember the indulgent smile with which she received my amazed wonder at the sheer perfection of stage management in the apprentice-scene in the *Meistersinger*, as she told me that they had had over fifty full rehearsals of it. As for her orthodoxy, she, with Hans Richter at her right hand, saw that everything, down to the smallest detail connected with the production, was done as *mein Mann* had ordained it. He had, for instance, allowed applause (otherwise *verboten*) at the conclusion of the last act of *Parsifal* on its first performance, and therefore ever afterwards the whole theatre resounded. He had permitted laughter at the battered Beckmesser's limpings and twinges in the third act of the *Meistersinger*, and thereafter the whole theatre exploded and rocked and guffawed, with the punctuality of a set fuse, at the appointed place, and then became instantly silent again. *Mein Mann* was her creed, and I have often seen her gently bow her grey head in reverence as she pronounced the sacred syllables. Indeed, being with Frau Cosima was like being in some consecrated building, and, as in church, one had to be very much on the guard against any hint of the ridiculous that might intrude into the solemnity, for such reactions are highly dangerous, and I was once, as follows, within an ace of irremediable disgrace.

The Master, as all the world knows, was buried in the back-garden at Wahnfried; an iron railing encloses the grave, which is situated in a shrubbery. Frau Cosima, on one fine, hot, windy morning, said she would take me to see the spot, and slowly pacing, like Gurnemanz and Parsifal, we entered a winding path and soon came in sight of the tomb. And then I thought I must have gone mad, for though it was a sultry August day, the grave at a distance appeared to be covered with snow. She did not seem to notice that, which made me more certain that I was in the grip of some outrageous hallucination. But as we approached, the wind puffed gustily, and the whole whiteness stirred and fluttered, and I saw that it was not snow at all, but calling-cards which the pilgrims habitually left there. There were hundreds of them, there were hundreds and thousands of them. I did not know that there were so many calling-cards in the world nor to how acid a test the need for gravity can be subjected. As we tottered away again, we met a party of pilgrims with their cards ready in their hands; the men, recognizing her, stopped and stood bareheaded as we passed, and all with downcast eyes and knitted brows of sympathetic sorrow, bowed and curtsied profoundly.

Once again, though less crucially, it was difficult to be quite solemn. I had been permitted to see the mechanisms in the theatre for the shifting of scenery and stage effects and lighting, and had examined the swings in which the Rhine-maidens dart and glide and poise as they flirt with Alberich (the motion of which, I was told, is very trying to the unaccustomed stomach, and often produces violent sea-sickness in the tuneful sirens until they get used to it). Then I had seen the cave from which Grane comes, the trap down which Erda goes, the cardboard Walhalla high above the rainbow bridge, the counterfeit Valkyries that scour the storm-clouds, the steam-breathing mask of the Worm, the Nibelungs' treasure, and Siegfried's bier. Just as we were looking reverently at that, Frau Cosima glided upon us, and with her own hand plucked a white calico rose from it and gave it me, and intoned the words, "I give it you off Siegfried's bier." . . . But this was Baireuth, and she was the Master's widow, already old and girt with an imperial dignity derived from the absolute sincerity of her own devotion, and bountifully fostered and fed by the incessant homage of adulatory pilgrims.

Most of those, all Germans certainly, who were privileged to be presented to her, bowed and curtsied and kissed her hand, and there she stood, handsome and rather horse-like, tossing her head slightly after she had bent it to a salutation, and it was all for the greater glory of *mein Mann*. So, indeed, was the entire township of Baireuth, for there was scarcely a shop-window, be it of plumber or confectioner, which did not show among its other wares, gilded plaster busts of the Master, and little Grails, like that in *Parsifal*, of metal or glass, to be purchased for a mark or two. There were Grails everywhere, some cheap, so as to be within reach of the poorest, others of more elaborate construction, made of lovely pink glass with a

MOTHER

gold line round the rim, and fitted with a battery and a button like an electric torch, so that when you pressed the button a light sprang up in the interior of the chalice, and it glowed beautifully, just as in the last act. There were little Siegfried-biers (at which now I could look quite untempted) and Klingsor-spears, and Parsifal-swans and Brünnhilde-horses, and Tarnhelms and Rings in such variety that you could have fitted yourself up with properties for a miniature marionette festival at home. Everywhere there were books of words, and arrangements of the music for the piano, and commentaries on the sacred text (for the Master, of course, wrote words as well as music), and photographs, photographs of the Master and the *Fest-spiel-haus*, and Wahnfried and the Grave, and Hans Richter and all the various artists in all their parts from Wotan and Parsifal down to the humblest Flower-maiden.

Never was there such wealth of suggestion : as you sauntered by the smelly river of a morning, whiling away the time till the opera began, you were all the time being hypnotized and made to believe that what you saw and heard in the *Fest-spiel-haus* was the final revelation of human genius (was it human ?). The festival was " run " with absolutely consummate skill : you heard and saw nothing but Wagner, you ate and drank Wagner, sacramentally almost and at considerable expense, because you had to dine between the acts at the restaurant outside the theatre, which, I fancy, was the property of the Wagners, and you rather rejoiced at the indescribable nastiness of the refreshment, because you felt that your swallowing of it was part of the treatment. Even your very uncomfortable lodging and the melancholy sanitary arrangements were ingredients in the prescription, joyfully imbibed, when at the conclusion of the opera, you made your way home, battered and dog-tired and enthusiastic, and stunned with music, and tumbled into a bed with a high watershed running longitudinally down the centre of it. The sheet was buttoned to the duvet, and the slightest movement after you had lain down, balancing yourself on the ridge of the water-shed, caused your clothes to roll off on one side and you on the other. . . . But something of the glory as well as the pain of martyrdom in the sacred cause accompanied these " fallings from you, vanishings," and it was Wagner who mingled in your uneasy hypnotized slumbers.

So, before the rise of Munich and the fall of Richter caused dusk to begin to gather on the slopes of Parnassus, the hypnotized, among them I cheerfully reckon myself, surrendered themselves completely to the spell. We allowed no spark of the critical spirit to glimmer, we firmly and faithfully shut our eyes to the numerous deficiencies in the performance. The orchestra was always magnificent, and never shall I forget a moment of true magic when Hans Richter was conducting the overture to the *Meistersinger*. It came with revelation and enlightenment, and while it lasted (a few bars) I was literally unaware in what terms the beauty of it was made manifest, whether it was a gleam of transcendent light that poured over the theatre, or the movement of some celestial, etheric wave that swept us along, or whether it was just the superb rendering of noble music. Magnificent, too, was the stage management: the crowds strolled and strayed, the apprentices danced like boys let out of school, the Rhine-maidens (when they had got used to the pitching) swayed and poised like mermaids in their own element, the storm in which the Valkyries assembled on the mountain-top was a miracle of atmospheric effect.

Again, there were (this year and the next) two or three first-rate singers there: Van Rooy played Wotan, and Ternina was a peerless Brünnhilde, but, with few exceptions, the singing was atrocious, and the appearance and acting of most of the characters unspeakable. Opera, that strange hybrid exotic art, makes its appeal to the eye hardly less than to the ear, and the eye was constantly shocked by deplorable sights, the ear outraged by shrieks, while the overflowings of German sentimentality revolted the mind. It was no wonder that Parsifal, an obese *roué*, failed to succumb to the mature charms of a barmaid who, for purposes of seduction, adopted the strange plan of talking to him about his deceased mother, or that the opening of monstrous magenta flowers, revealing yet more monstrous maidens, left him morally impregnable. Again, in the *Meistersinger*, Walther was not a tenor at all, nor yet a young impassioned Ritter; he was a bellowing baritone of portly habit, employed on a middle-aged flirtation with a bulging *haus-frau*. Yet, in the hypnotic state, you firmly shut eyes and ears to all such blemishes, and even when Grane, a mild and spavined cob, was led out of his cave by Brünnhilde, and, refusing to proceed, did what no stage direction ordained, we sat with grave eyes downcast till Grane was comfortable. Not a titter, not a tremor was heard, and this unrehearsed effect we never alluded to afterwards. Entirely hypnotized, we took whatever was vouchsafed us with a greedy gusto, accepting the suggestion that before us was It, the Alpha and Omega in the history of celestial music-drama. Some interior voice, like an *enfant terrible*, occasionally protested that this was a ghastly goitred crew of gods and goddesses, who could not sing, who could not act, who could only storm and strut and rage and melt, but it was instantly silenced, as with a hand laid over its mouth, by the knowledge that this was Baireuth and that every wooden gesture and piercing scream, every obesity and rotundity, was as the Master had ordained. We bowed our heads before *mein Mann*.

Of course, there was a splendour about it, the splendour of the magnificent rendering of the orchestral score, and of the enthusiastic conviction which permeated the vast and reverent crowd that everything was " apparelled in celestial light." But the splendour owed much to suggestion, to the tacit understanding that you must no more question or criticize, if you were worthy to come to Baireuth at all, than a Christian may dispute the dogmas on which his faith rests, for if he does, he is no longer a Christian. At the end, I remember being bidden to a musical party at Wahnfried, at which I supposed we should have nothing but the Master's music. But, contrary to expectation, we had not a bar of the Master's music: there was Bach, there was Handel, there was something Italian. Is it fanciful to suppose that this was a sort of vaccination, administered when we were leaving Baireuth and going out into the world again, to render us immune in an atmosphere charged with the poisonous microbes of other music? Wagner's spirit seemed to preside over this precautionary concert: almost I saw him hovering in the shadows, dressed in his broadcloth and loose tie, or, better still, in his velvet jacket and Tam-o'-shanter, or, best of all, in the flowered dressing-gown, smiling at the throng of patients who were being made safe. Rich velvet curtains, with cords and tassels, were drawn over the windows to exclude any particle of air that was not charged with Wagnerismos: the opulent wallpaper was gay with mirrors framed in plush and painted with lilies; there were saddle-bag sofas and gildings, and shiny brown woods and inlaid mantelpieces which looked like brawn, and a pair of stupendous porcelain vases presented (and I should conjecture designed) by the All Highest, and everywhere, everywhere pictures and photographs of the Master. How scrannel sounded the strains of Handel and of Bach! We should be safe from infection till we met at Baireuth again.

I must have been extremely young for my three and thirty years when, in the autumn of 1900, I set up a flat of my independent own, or else I was over-ripe for freedom, for the fact of complete freedom went straight to my head, and life became an orgy, a whirl of enthusiasms and experiments. My vaccination at Baireuth had not taken very well, for in music I at once succumbed to an attack of Queen's Hall measles, and for a little the Tschaikowsky night, once a week at the Promenade Concerts, was as delirious as the Wagner night. I am not sure that we had nothing but Tschaikowsky on these nights, but there would at least be a symphony, and the Casse Noisette, or the 1912 Overture, or the piano concerto, and what everyone who claimed to be up to date in musical taste prized most of all, was the $\frac{5}{4}$ movement in the sixth symphony. For a while, amazing as it sounds, that was the last word, the supreme utterance, and those who had (and who had not?) the Tschaikowsky measles, whistled the $\frac{5}{4}$ movement, and picked it out on the piano, and knew that there was no more to be said. And who could conduct the $\frac{5}{4}$ movement like Mr. Henry Wood? He made curious dancing movements, as in some hieratic cake-walk: he made superb side-strokes as in swimming with one arm, and stabs as with a rapier with the other. He crept, he slid, he raged, he cossetted and coaxed and cajoled, and the band was one with the emotion that possessed him. Indeed, it was quite a shock when Hans Richter gave the same music at a symphony concert, for when he came to the $\frac{5}{4}$ he just collected his orchestra on the end of his baton, gave one beat, and then turned his back on them and faced the house, while they played it precisely as they played it when Mr. Wood danced before them.

Indeed, we who were so fortunate as to be young and much alive in the nineties, and the year or two before and after, had an astonishing number of measles to catch, by which I mean this sudden succumbing, as in mild childish illnesses, to some new phenomenon in art or letters which seemed at the moment to be a "last word." From the noble diseases one is never immune, for the man who ever ceases to suffer, so to speak, from Bach, is musically moribund. But there are others, Fauré perhaps, and Debussy, and, I hope, Stravinski, who represent measles, which infect one for a time, "come out" in a violent rash with fever, and, subsiding, are afterwards powerless to inflame again the individual who has experienced them. And in those years there was so much being produced in many lines that was apt to attack you as with fever; so much that arrested and challenged you. So many new notes were sounded, so many mornings gilded the hill-tops, and while some eager adventurers passionately averred that now at last true day was dawning, others with equal passion were sure that these strange lights were not of the wholesome sun, nor even of a borrowing moon, but of fatuous fires in the marsh of decadence.

It was in the nineties (with the margin of a year or two on each side) that Mr. Kipling invented India, made poets out of privates, and revealed to the British the empire of their birthright, that Mrs. Humphry Ward caused Robert Elsmere to undermine the foundations of Christian belief, that the Yellow Book appeared with the finest work which Aubrey Beardsley ever did, and which, when it first appeared, seemed epoch-making, as no doubt for a little while it was. Then Beardsley turned author and made the Savoy magazine blush with his tale of " Under the Hill." In those lively and experimental days Mr. Henry James was confounding his earlier admirers, who read and re-read *Roderick Hudson* and *The Portrait of a Lady* with unspeakable reverence, and was raising up armies of new readers, who took the place of the old brigades who fell stark and staring beneath the stroke of *The Wings of the Dove*. Stevenson, in Samoa, was fertile with romances of Scotland and the South Seas, and to us then *Tess of the D'Urbervilles* was a milestone of modern realism, which earlier Victorians passed with averted gaze and with horror to see how far they had travelled. George Meredith was still writing, and occasionally from Putney there came melodies in the authentic lyrical voice. Mr. H. G. Wells was bringing out his first fascinating stories about time-machines and invisible men, and a hush would fall on polite circles if mention was made of *Esther Waters*.

Then at the theatre you could see Sarah Bernhardt and Eleanora Dusé, the one before the decline from the zenith of her power, the other just reaching it, and Henry Irving and Ellen Terry were at the Lyceum, and Mrs. Patrick Campbell was making the earliest of her triumphs at the St. James's. Then, too, Oscar Wilde was producing the plays which, however artificial they may seem now, sent his audiences reeling into the street, intoxicated by epigram and paradox. None of them had the smallest spark of immortality, except possibly *The Importance of Being Earnest*, but they were new, and their audacious nonsense was very like wit. Wit, indeed, he had, but it was conversational wit, that gleamed and vanished before the shallowness or profundity of it steadily revealed itself. Even in conversation he was not the equal of Whistler for incisive penetration, nor for intellectual charm of Mr. Edmund Gosse. Then came his sudden and tragic catastrophe; the jury could not agree at the first trial, and with savage stupidity a second trial was ordered. The procedure was savage, because he was already completely disgraced, and could never have continued to live in England: it was stupid because it and the relentless sentence that followed were construed into a sort of martyrdom in countries where he could not for such offences have been prosecuted at all. It was for that far more than for the intrinsic merits of his achievements in art that the *culte* for him as a writer and dramatist began, which has since swelled to such vast proportions on the Continent. Strauss composed an opera on his *Salome*, which the censor had banned in England on the eve of its production by Sarah Bernhardt, and his works ran into as many editions as before they had sold copies. To that also we owe *The Ballad of Reading Gaol*, which, in spite of its obvious indebtedness to other poems, is one of the finest ballads in our language.

In those excited days, too, people argued about Mr. Sargent, and said they would not like to be painted by him because he brought out all that was "horrid" in his sitter, and Whistler was still largely considered to be a charlatan or a buffoon, and he, proving himself as subtle with the pen as the paint-brush, delighted us with *The Gentle Art of Making Enemies*, in case his amazing libel action against Professor Ruskin should perish from men's minds. And if you did not like Whistler's prose, you could read a new romance by Miss Marie Corelli, and if you did not like his pictures, you could go to see the Doré gallery, which was a little less subtle. And at the pantomime were Dan Leno and Herbert Campbell, and there was a skating-rink where the panorama of Niagara had been, and there were beautiful horses and carriages in the Park, instead of mephitic motor-cars, and, oh, what interesting and wonderful people sat inside them!

It is very hard to get the present and the past of twenty years ago into true perspective, if, indeed, there is any such thing as true perspective. The foreground, the present, in any matter of reminiscences, is apt to become smaller than it really is, while the past, the background, tends to become magnified as by some sort of mirage, and gleam with a more vivid opalescence than it possessed at the time. It is very hard, in fact, to be sure that you are right, when you say " there were giants in those days," and though all those who were intelligently conscious then are agreed on the correctness of their measurements, that is no proof that they are right: they may be the victims of collective hallucination. But you cannot excavate (as we did in Egypt) for evidence of what took place in the nineties, and impressions are the only source of information, though possibly a fallacious one. And it appears to me that even more than in this matter of art and letters (making due allowance for measles), the significant public figures of those days were on a larger scale than are the significant figures of to-day to either the young or the middle-aged. Loyalty to the throne, for instance, is just as fervent to-day as it was thirty years ago, but it is idle to pretend that when King George visits an institution or unveils a statue there is the thrill with which in the nineties we lined the streets to see Queen Victoria pass. There she sat, little and aged and huddled, with the black parasol and the tired bulging eyes, and there was awe. What was it composed of? Perhaps it partly arose from the rarity of her appearances, and from the fact that she was so little and so old, and seemed so lonely and was so immense, but there was something else. Or, when, lately, we saw Mr. Lloyd George, with the weight of the empire at war on his shoulders, marching to the House of Commons, distinguished if ever man was by the most perilous burden man has ever borne, we did not gaze, as we gazed on Lord Salisbury, in mild and uneventful times, struggling with his tricycle in St. James's Park. The crowd does not stand a-gape to see Mr. Baldwin stepping into his motor-car, with the glow of gratification in which it beheld Mr. Gladstone storming a hansom-cab. It may be that the new age has not got the sense of reverence, but why should the older generation have lost it and cannot find in contemporary phenonema the distinction of the past?

As for " Society " (to use a dreadful term of which nobody quite knows the meaning, except, presumably, the people who talk about it), it was extremely like what it always has been and always will be. For " Society "—to guess at its connotation—has always been a thing of the past, something brilliant and exclusive, which has now gone to the dogs. Or at least the cats have got it. Certainly in the nineties there were plenty of folk (just as there are now) who moaned that there was no Society any longer: "Look at the women: look at their dresses! They would never have got into Society in my day. Why my mother——" But then, at every epoch since Society invented itself the same cry has been raised. Compare, for instance, in this matter of women's dress (which appears to be much involved in the mysterious term), what Lady William Wynn (Charlotte Greville) wrote to a friend in 1826, with what the *Evening Standard* said in 1920 on the same everlasting subject. Here is Lady William's comment: "All the fine ladies have tucked up their petticoats to *mi-jambe*, and I believe they are still on the ascent. So true it is that, sometimes at one end, sometimes at the other, Eve's petticoat is nearly all that remains unliable to curtailment."

And here is the *Evening Standard's* comment in 1920: "Apparently, to be fashionable in these days, a piece of material about the size of a couple of dinner-napkins is considered to be quite sufficient to make a becoming ball-gown."

Or take the complaint current to-day that there is no such thing as conversation, that an after-dinner reception where there is not dancing or bridge or music is no longer possible. Precisely the same moan was raised in the nineties when bridge began to take hold. Those who did not play bridge, said that this infernal game had killed conversation, while those who did, said that there was no conversation to kill. . . . And the cigarette habit killed the leisurely discussion of port, just as port killed the finer appreciation of claret. Society has always just had its throat cut and is squealing with approaching dissolution. And then, as now, people bawled across the dinner-table concerning " tips " on the Stock Exchange (only they bawled about South African gold-fields then, and Mexican oil now), and concerning diseases and God and adultery, and other people blanched, then as now, at the demise of decency. Others, again, turned up their eyes until only the whites were visible at the invasion of the sacred precincts of aristocratic Society by the wives of pork-butchers with pearls, who came to London because they were not received by the élite of Chicago, and of Semites who were nobodies in Jerusalem, as if on one of the days of creation the command had gone forth, " Let there be a British aristocracy," and there was a British aristocracy, which was both the greater light that ruled the day, and the lesser light that ruled the night. These purists quite forgot that the process had always been going on, and that the venerable and magnificent families of to-day had not so very long ago been parvenus who had made money as merchants and shopkeepers and business men, or were the bastards of nobler lines. The process has always been at work in every century and every decade, and decent Society has always been in its death-agony.

Then, too, as now, there were precisely the same sets and cliques and coteries and climbers, and some were intellectual, and some artistic, and some were supposed to pay a good deal of attention to their souls, and if they were a little priggish, and mistook priggishness for profundity and gabbling for genius, they enjoyed it very much, and so did everybody else; and, of course, there was a Smart Set, so-called by those who, not being in it, despised it, and then, as now, there were musical sets who gasped at long-haired Russian pianists, who had never been heard before and were never heard of again. Probably there was rather less over-lapping in the nineties than there is now, for there were sharper lines of demarcation between different sets then, and no European war had jumbled everybody up together in a macedoine, which will require a great deal of sorting-out, if the lines of demarcation are to return.

But, if that happens, there will be found missing

in the jig-saw puzzle of it all, a certain " piece " which in the nineties was the centre and clue. Behind and below these shifting surfaces, there was then a body of people who owned land and had nice English names, and were rich and simple, and were the greatest and most magnificent of hosts and hostesses. They had large estates in the country (not oil-wells or gold-mines) where they were kind and considerate landlords, and big houses in town, where they exercised a national and splendid hospitality : there was a stateliness, a scale, a breeding, a certain code of manners. I hold no brief for it, I make myself a looker-on, but I can assert, without fear of contradiction, that it no longer is the source from which Society springs.

From a chronicler's point of view, its elusiveness to definition lies in the fact that it is impossible to describe it in positive terms, saying what it was, but only in negative terms, saying what it was not. In the main, what it was not was a scurry. Women—those who were of it—did not dine at restaurants, and waggle their hands to friends at neighbouring tables, and wonder who was she with pearls by the window, and send a note to an acquaintance to find out. They dined at home, or at the houses of their friends, and had no need to ask who anybody was, because they already knew. During dinner they did not, about pudding-time, put a bag on the table and take out a cigarette-case and powder their noses, nor did they beg people whom they had never seen before to stay with them, because they had heard that they were "killing," nor did they go anywhere that they were asked in order to get a dinner and a place in an opera-box and a lift home without expense, and most emphatically they did not, for value received, launch the unknown rich, crockery-kings and silver-kings and railway-kings and lavatory-kings, in Society. I do not mean that in the nineties, just as much as now, there were not many, who ought to have known better, who did such things, but there was then a large body of well-bred people in the world that amused itself, who did not bend the knee to Baal, and were, at the same time, the people who "mattered." Of course there were climbers in the nineties, as in every other age, and they climbed with no less agility than now into the smartest situations, but there were more places then from which they slipped back as down a greased pole. The climbers came more croppers. . . .

The manners of those who belonged to this Society, which was not a clique, or a set, or anything of the kind, had an appropriate reticence and restraint. They could be jovial and noisy enough among their own friends, but they did not squeal in public. Men had a certain "behaviour" with women, and women with men. There are plenty of men and women to-day who are of precisely the same breed and distinction as they: the difference is that they are no longer the leaders and lavish entertainers of the town. Twenty years of growing taxation and burden to land-owners have impoverished them, and in any case they were not of the stuff which competitors are made of, that tough, pushing, knock-down-the-ladder breed that now crow on the tree-tops. These others had nowhere to climb to, they were there already.

One evening in particular remains very vivid in my mind as characteristic of "that sort of thing." The hostess was the late Lady Ripon (then Countess de Grey), who perhaps, above all others, was typical of a kind of hospitality which has vanished. She combined all the gifts and brilliances with which a woman can be endowed: she was wonderfully beautiful, she had wit and distinction, and a certain splendour now completely obsolete. She gave a small evening-party one night at her little house in Bruton Street, and among her guests, royal and otherwise, there came Édouard and Jean de Reszke. They had both of them just sung at the closing night of the opera, and Lady de Grey, just for fun, said to Édouard "Won't you sing something?" And he with alacrity replied, "Certainly I will: I have never sung in so small a room." He then sang the "Veau d'Or" from *Faust* at the top of his voice, and the windows rattled and the floor shook. This encouraged Jean, who said, "Now I will sing: I will show you how I sing the 'Preisleid.'" And he stood in the middle of the room, rather precariously, on two footstools, and gave the most inimitable parody of himself singing Walther's song in the *Meistersinger*. Probably he sang that more magnificently than it has ever been sung, but now, in his best manner and his best voice, he made it hopelessly ludicrous. . . . And then Réjane (just for fun) recited "La Poupée."

But even then, apart from taxation and its impoverishments, there were already solvents at work which were disintegrating their supremacy, and, curiously enough, the most powerful of those solvents came, not from without, but from within. Most potent of all the influences that undermined them was that of Edward VII, then Prince of Wales. As a bulwark of the throne and of the constitution he strenuously upheld them, but he wanted sometimes to get away from thoughts of throne, and be a private gentleman amusing himself. Probably they, too, were a little too conscious of his identity, and, in consequence, they were not his idea of relaxation when the foundation-stones were laid, and the docks opened, and his duties done. His close personal friends were not in the main among them. He liked something a little more ununiformed, so to speak, when he was no longer impersonating Britannia, something more unfetteredly festive, a joke that had to be whispered, a game of baccarat, an informality, a practical joke, in which somebody fell down, or found an egg in his pyjamas, or experienced other quaint happenings. These laudable and laughable devices were a reasonable relaxation, an escape from the burden of his Heir-apparency and its attendant ceremony. He sought a discreet cosmopolitan privacy for his amusement, when he need not be dignified, though when dignity was indicated, nobody was ever more so. There is a story that he was staying once at a great house, which might be considered a little over-starched, and that on his arrival in the drawing-room after dinner his hostess frankly told him that she did not allow cards in her house, but that there was a gramophone. Like a great gentleman he listened to the gramophone, and politely marvelled at the strides science had made.

The nineties and the remaining fourteen years that preceded the war have, probably rightly, earned the distinction of having attained, in the matter of general extravagance in entertainment and amusement, the apex of sheer squander. Nowadays nobody English has the same amount of money to throw about, but, apart from that, the diminished scale is largely due to the discovery that it is possible to enjoy yourself equally well on less. Ten people, it has been detected, can amuse themselves from Saturday till Monday in the country as successfully as thirty, the air need not be black with pheasants to ensure a good day's shooting, and, above all, a sufficiency of delicious food is as pleasant as an interminable succession of dishes which nobody wants. There is, of course, nothing ascetic or self-denying in being content without the things you do not in the least desire, and in spite of the optimism of those who say that the war has made us simpler and more serious, it does not need a war to produce a simplicity which only dispenses with what we have found we do not care about : such a thing might happen without a war. Acrobatic aspirants to social distinction naturally will always bait their hooks with pearls of the Orient if they think that by such enticements they will induce the great fish to swallow them as well as the pearls, but, apart from these, there would seem to be more sense nowadays than during those sumptuous years in the paraphernalia of entertainment and in the diversions of domestic life. It would, for instance, in these more economical days be difficult to find anyone, however rich, emulating the ingenious expenditure of Mr. Alfred de Rothschild, who, when he was quietly at home at Halton, perhaps with one or two guests in the house, or perhaps with none at all but his attendant doctor, used often to sit on Sunday morning at a small circus of his own devising. There was a miniature grandstand, and a stable and a track, and when all was ready the *écuyer* would crack his whip and there trotted in a couple of ponies, which had a friendly little race, and when it was done looked for a lump of sugar. When the thrill of that passed off, some dogs, ridden by jockeying monkeys, sometimes cantered round; diminutive hurdles were erected and a depressed rabbit lolloped over them. . . . And could we to-day find such a Lucullus as he who once asked a friend of mine to share his pot-luck? There were just the two of them, and when a slice of boiled turbot emerged from the pot, a spoonful of lobster-sauce accompanied it. The sauce seemed excellent, and my friend politely extolled it. "You shall have the recipe," said this amiable Lucullus, and up it came, and was handed to him. It began, "Lobster-sauce for two. Take seven hen lobsters." . . . *Ichabod, ichabod!*

This same Lucullus suffered from a congestion of the liver, for the hen-lobsters were vindictive dames. His doctor ordered him gentle horse-exercise, but told him that he ought not to get wet, or to incur undue fatigue. He, therefore, took mild rides, and sometimes went to have tea with a cousin of his, riding his horse as ordered, with a groom in attendance. But the groom could not control the weather, so a neat, two-horsed brougham followed the groom, in case, after they had started, the afternoon turned out wet. Nor could the groom control a feeling of fatigue on the part of his master, who would not, if he felt tired, want to go home in a brougham when the sun was shining, but would like to enjoy the air. So a pony-carriage followed the brougham. I was staying with this cousin of his on one of the occasions that Lucullus thought he could manage a ride of about two miles, and have tea with her.

He brought over a friend with him, for whom he provided the same equipment, and thus it happened that when I came back after a stroll, I saw drawn up at the front-door two pony carriages and two broughams, while two grooms held the heads of four horses. Allowing two people for each brougham, and each pony-carriage, and one for each horse, I expected to find twelve guests within. But there were only two. Sometimes, when in London, he used to walk in the Park, and then only the brougham followed him.

But however extravagant England was in those fat years of prosperity, it never really rivalled the imbecilities of America, nor, though from time to time our Transatlantic cousins have given us treats in the way of those " freak " parties which there seem to be the test of social brilliance, has that particular form of idiotic entertainment taken root here. Is it that we are lacking in a sense of humour, and do not see how exquisitely witty it is to turn a house into an Indian jungle, and give a dinner-party for a hundred and fifty guests, whose wants are attended to by a host of waiters from a respectable catering establishment, who have been induced by enhanced pay to wear a species of toga instead of trousers and to swathe their Saxon heads in turbans ? Such bids for

MOTHER

social sovereignty have been occasionally made here, at which, between the courses of dinner, amazing things have been devised to *épater* this *bourgeois* London : a sedan-chair has appeared, out of which stepped a skinny young lady, naked except for an exiguous loin-cloth, but gilded all over from head to foot, who proceeded to dance in a voluptuous manner. Lottery tickets in another interval were handed round, and everyone carried away something expensive, or a cake perhaps was cut which proved to be full of gold cigarette-cases and jewelled ornaments, and then the young lady came back, without her gilding, and danced again.... But somehow such strokes of genius in hospitality have never had any great success here : they seem rather to be matters to which the attention of the Commissioners in Lunacy should be directed.

It was into this world of entertainment and friendly folk that I leaped, panting in the hot chase of enchanting occupation, and as strenuous in the pursuit of pastimes as if each was the object of life. If I came into my flat at timeless hours, that was only a matter between my latchkey and me, and I invented, if I was aware that it was abnormally near morning, a most pleasing device to test my self-control. This consisted in winding up my watch with small and uneven twirlings and a detached mind, so that I could not guess how near it was to running down, and in then going to bed without a glance at its accusing dial. No one who has not tried has any idea how difficult this is to do, so intense is the desire, either to know the full measure of your shame or to assure yourself that it is not so late after all. Indeed, the hours of the day and night alike were all too short for me, so that by day I would fain have been Joshua to bid the sun stand still, and by night I muttered Ovid's prayer, "*O, lente, lente, currite noctis ejus,*" which in the vulgar tongue means, "It can't be morning yet."

For there was so much to do, so much ready and toasted and buttered, quite apart from the real business of my life, of which I shall subsequently speak. By day I had to skate so much at Niagara, being at that time quite sure that life would never attain its full fruition until I had passed all three tests of the National Skating Association (English style), and could wear a badge of pure gold (silver and copper discarded) in my buttonhole. So the whole morning would be spent, like the aspiring Christian, with "the frequent fall," and I would hobble away to lunch with entrancing people and go back for the afternoon skating session (session it was!) at three, and skate till it was almost a relief to hear the gong announce closing-time. And then I hobbled home, and went out to dinner and bridge, and midnight and the small hours, and an exercise of self-control, sometimes successful. Next morning, with more self-control, I would perhaps study a novel instead of skating. That does not sound very serious, but for me it was, owing to my profession. For I did not read novels casually, with a view to entertainment, in an arm-chair, but in order to find out how to tell stories: how it should be done, and how it should not be done.

Then, as if I had not sufficient diversion already, and was not earning sufficient money to defray the expenses of a reasonably luxurious existence, I plunged into a disastrous course of optimistic speculation on the Stock Exchange, and very soon got rid of such monies as I had already invested in dull debentures and sound stock: "Get poor quick" seems to have been my motto and device. There was a boom going on in Australian gold-mines about this time, and thinking that a gift for finance was one of my undiscovered qualities, I proceeded to prove, by wild investment in amazing companies, that it was not.

There was a mine called Lady Loch, and another

called Lady Shenton, and I began by loading their seductive ladyships with my devout, though modest, offerings. Then, launching out a little more boldly, I bought Golden Links, and Chaffers, and Great Boulder Main Reef, and with a puckered brow, when the *Financial Times* recorded a disagreeable lack of professional confidence in their prospects, I dived into the Oxford Street tube (for the sake of saving a cab-fare), and burrowing into the City, I communed with my broker on the causes of this sad scepticism. He was a circular Dutch broker, obese and optimistic, and not only did I consider him to have a very remarkable financial gift, so winningly did he talk about refractory ores, and tailings and assays and the cyanide process, but he seemed to regard me as a promising nephew whose abilities he held in great respect, and he was pleased to see me exercising them so industriously. He gave me attractive reasons (all the more alluring because they were slightly unintelligible) why Golden Links were temporarily tarnished and now worth considerably less than when he had bought them for me, and thought that I could not do better than buy some more at a lower price in order to " average." Thus, if I had originally paid £4 for each Golden Link, and it was now only worth £2, I had better purchase an equal number at £2, so that when they went up to £3, I should see my money back again, and any further rise would be pure gain. This was admirable reasoning, but it left out of the question where I should be if they went lower yet, which they invariably did. . . .

The worst drawback about being concerned in such money-making schemes as Golden Links, was that it resembled being in an express train, for Golden Links moved so fast (in a retrograde direction) that I never could summon up the nerve to jump out before the crash. Other wares, too, my broker had, which might in comparison be called gilt-edged, for though they always declined in value, they did so quite slowly, and you had plenty of time to disembark. . . . You may wonder how I could be so silly, and I am sure I wonder too (perhaps I had better have given a " freak " party with all that money), but then, if we were wise, what would happen to all these gentlemen in the City ? And, after all, I had diversion and excitement, for I never ceased to think that I was about to pull money out of those holes in the ground in West Australia. And since, when I " averaged," I had not got to take bright shining sovereigns out of my pocket, but only instruct my broker to sell out other and firmer investments, there was no sense of impoverishment. To lose a couple of pounds at bridge was discouraging, because I had to part with gold pieces, but the absence of some certificate at the Bank was hardly noticeable. Besides, I learned the habit of travelling in tubes on those repeated visits to the City, and that has since saved me a great many shillings. . . .

Eventually all these vigorous concerns blossomed into reconstructions involving heavy calls, and then faded away into abysmal dimness and darkness. They were Snarks: "they softly and silently vanished away," and some awakening to the light of common day and common sense, scattered my feverish financial dreamings. I dabbled no more in that bright but perilous sea, and snowed all future communications from my kind, expensive Dutch uncle into the waste-paper basket.

CHAPTER VI

AMONG all these shifting hobbies and distractions I had one fixed pursuit, that of learning how to write novels, and, with the object of finding out, I read novels in prodigious quantities to see " how it was done." I studied styles and methods, and this account of my study, therefore, is a chapter of mere shop.

I began with English classics, which had form and technique, and told their story in an orderly manner (in consequence of which nobody ever reads them now), and read about half of Dickens through, omitting books like *David Copperfield*, of which I could already have written a detailed analysis, and those like *Pickwick*, which would yield none. While enormously admiring, I thought that his gigantic canvases were too completely in focus: they were like Mr. Frith's famous picture of Derby Day. They were detailed chronicles of the divers lives of many amusing and terrible characters, whose interests and adventures, it is true, crossed and were interwoven, but did not contribute to a conflagration, for which the author should have been piling the fuel all along, and which at the end would flare into flame. There seemed only one exception, that of Edwin Drood, where clearly some tremendous climax was being built from the very first page and with so stealthy a hand that no one has hazarded a successful guess what that climax would have been.

But then, Dickens did not mean to have a climax in my sense : that was his way of doing it. I hated the sentimentality of little Nell and Paul Dombey and Smike and Tiny Tim and Ruth Pinch, and we must have none of that in the Great Work (which still abides unwritten), nor yet so heaven-sent a genius as Nicholas Nickleby, who, without having learned anything about acting, found it perfectly easy to play Romeo to an entranced audience, and to teach the idiotic Smike to be " the prince and paragon of apothecaries." But Nicholas, when greatly moved, spoke blank verse, which showed an abnormal brain, since most people when greatly moved become incoherent and ejaculatory. . . . I did not, however, pay much attention to Dickens's faults, and, not being a reviewer, what I was looking for was his merits, and, sure, there were merits enough in the astounding vitality of his creations. True, you never in actual life met with any human being who resembled any of his intense personages, and that was the supreme merit, they were types and distillations, the broth of inebriated parsons, the elixir of stage-coach drivers, the brandy of water-rate collectors.

At the other end of the classical spectrum was Jane Austen, any of whose characters (allowing for the slight change superficially wrought by the lapse of eighty years) you might meet round the next corner. They were no less typical than the creations of Dickens, but, by an art elusive and impeccable, were ordinary individuals as well. Mrs. Gaskell was a wizard of similar spells, and Trollope (though his spells sometimes produced only a little milk and water), and George Eliot. But to me the greatest wizard of all was Emily Brontë: how many times I have read *Wuthering Heights* I have no idea, but never, in spite of the clumsiness of its narration, have I laid it down without the firm conviction that it stands alone at the head of all novels in the English language.

I swam ashore out of the classical seas and plunged into the rapids of recent and contemporary work, where (thoroughly to mix my metaphors) I caught all manner of measles. I had long been sick with (not of) Stevenson, and now, still seriously ill, I read his romances and short stories through, with the exception of *The Black Arrow*, over which I joined hands with his wife. I read, too, all I could about him; I pored over the *Vailima Letters*; I devoured every crumb that fell from the tables of those who had known him: I treasured whatever anybody else said about him, and what he said about himself, and cordially agreed when he told Mr. Colvin [1] that if he had only written the story of " Tod Lapraik " and " Thrawn Janet " he would still be a great author. I would sooner have heard that the conclusion of *Weir of Hermiston* had been found, than that a fourth synoptist had been discovered.

And then my fever, most unexpectedly, began to subside, and I think the febrifuge must have been contained in the large doses of Mr. George Moore which I was beginning to take. I found myself less delirious and able to try to form some opinion of my own about his books, instead of reading them with the postulate that they were perfect, and, if necessary, revising my notions of perfection by their standard. The light of common day and common sense in place of that which never was on sea or land began to break the spell that held me uncritically captive.

[1] Mr. Colvin, and many of the illustrious folk of whom I make mention, have since become knights and other sumptuousnesses, but I allude to them as they then were.

How I clung to my measles and hated to see the rash and the temperature subside! I repeated to myself long pieces out of *Jekyll and Hyde*, I murmured as I walked down Oxford Street such sentences as "dabbling with dishes in a bedroom may make clean the body, but the imagination takes no share in such a cleansing." I re-read the flight in the heather out of *Kidnapped*, and I began more anxiously to consider what Stevenson had told us and how he had told it. Was there (in a whisper) just a hint of journalese in that careful and studied style? Would Mr. George Moore have said "threatened him with corporalities"; would he not have said more simply and quite as effectively "told him he'd smack his head"? And would not Mr. George Moore have said "imitated" or "copied," instead of "played the sedulous ape"? Was it a literary "score" to say "played the sedulous ape"? I felt I could safely untie myself from the mast without fear of throwing myself overboard to the sweet singing of the sirens, Mr. Sidney Colvin and Mr. Andrew Lang. I worshipped at this shrine no longer; indeed, the most robust literary digestion could scarcely assimilate Stevenson and Mr. George Moore simultaneously. To chew the one, it was necessary to eschew the other, and now I was busy masticating *The Confessions of a Young Man*. Mr. Moore contemplated himself from all quarters, as in one of those ingenious looking-glasses with adjustable wings, which show you profile, full face, and three-quarter face. Mr. Moore's looking-glass was of full length, and in its magical surface you beheld every bit of Mr. Moore, front and back, in all possible aspects. The interesting image was unerringly reflected in the smooth and tranquil art of his style, and I felt that I knew exactly all that Mr. Moore desired his readers to know about himself, and what a lot that was! He took you to his bedroom and muttered, " Now I will show you what I am."

And then with mounting fever I read *Esther Waters*, and I felt I was quite right to admire it so much for its simple and economical craftsmanship, for Mr. Moore has told us that he admired it too. He was just as wonderful when he fell on his friends Mr. Yeats and Lady Gregory, and pulled them in front of his magic looking-glass and made them appear precisely as he wished them to appear. (I think, perhaps, he wrote about them later on; I am sure I do not remember, but the point is that sooner or later he did write about them, and I read it.)

It must have been subsequently, also, that I read his memories of his dead life, which was wonderfully alive. And though I wished that Mr. Moore had not said to the young lady whom he took to Orelay, "Wilful Doris! Pretty Puss-cat"; and that when he alluded to Beethoven's Appasionata, he did not call it the "Impassionata," I never really cared what Mr. Moore said, so long as he went on saying it. And how I wanted to know whether the literary lady from Texas became a mother. . . .

A golden rule I learned from Mr. Moore, and that was to make up my mind precisely as to what I meant to say, and then precisely to say it. What a great writer I should have been if I had been capable of that, for all sorts of interesting things came into my head, but I could not state them with precision!

After Mr. Moore, I thought it would be nice to get out-of-doors, and I plunged into *The Forest Lovers* of Mr. Hewlett. But to my dismay I could not see the wood for the trees, and never have I been so disconcerted. I could not get on: I stuck fast in the mire where no ground is; I was like a fly that before it has begun to eat the honey finds that it is no longer able to move.

It was most humiliating, for I felt sure that Mr.

Hewlett might have taught me such a lot about style and method, if I only had been able to read what he wrote. I tried all the devices: I began first at the beginning of his book, and then I began in the middle, hoping to find such gems there that I should make light of the task of mining for them, and then I tried the end, and then I shut it up. After that I read something by Mr. Barrie, which made me understand what perfect ladies and gentlemen the Scotch are, and so sly and witty, and then I read *The Manxman* by Mr. Hall Caine. That was a prodigious book, delivered with Sinaitic solemnity and circumstance. It was full of fire and thunderstorms and tempests and trumpets, and I quite understood how it was that, if the people on the Isle of Man are like that, the cats have no tails, for anything so flippant as a tail could not possibly exist on the same island as Mr. Hall Caine. I felt that I had gone up Sinai with Mr. Hall Caine, and had heard *The Manxman* dictated to him out of the cloud, and had seen him carve it all on stone tables. He brought them down with him, not the least staggering under their weight, and translated it into all the European languages and published the versions simultaneously with photographs of himself and accounts of how it all came to him.

It was grand, and I was so taken up with the grandeur that I could never remember what it was about. But I learned from it that it is possible to produce and arrange and marshal, as in a procession, a most amazing amount of material, so that it passes before the reader in a manner as orderly as one of Mr. Louis Parker's pageants. . . .

And I read some vigorous books by Miss Marie Corelli, and subsequently visited her at Stratford-on-Avon, where I saw the pen with which she wrote *The Sorrows of Satan.*

I omitted to read Meredith, because I knew he defied analysis, and went on to Mr. H. G. Wells, who was then weaving the most wonderful stories about men from Mars, and men in the moon, and a machine that could push Time forward through lapses of uncounted æons, and show us the earth growing cold. Possibly, if M. Jules Verne had never written his entrancing tales, we should never have had Mr. Wells's, which only made me grateful to M. Jules Verne for having done so, and how I revelled in the direct lucidity of his style: he said just what he meant to say, like Mr. George Moore. Mr. Wells, in that felicitous period, had not awoke to any sense of his mission, nor wanted to rearrange the world on a wholly different plan, nor had he yet discovered God and Anne Veronica, and I wish he could have gone on dreaming his sumptuous nightmares. But he awoke. . . .

Indeed, there seemed to be as many methods as there were Masters, but as I emerged from this sea of fiction, I found that a certain fluid belief of mine had now been churned by study into the solid conviction that the only sure method of revealing your characters in fiction is by their direct speech, and the certainty of that outweighed all else that I had learned. No amount of discussion or comment or analysis on the part of the author will ever give any of his puppets the vividness and reality which the puppet himself can create when he talks. " Out of the heart the mouth speaketh " has no truer application than in the world of fiction. Sincerity, pomposity, simplicity, love, honour, rascality, and all the gamut of qualities, are far more trenchantly conveyed by direct speech than by action, paradoxical though it sounds, and though it may not be applicable to the world where conduct is supposed to be nine parts of life. Yet even action is better than mere analysis, for the more you only dissect, the more indubitably dead your subject becomes. A large school of modern fiction is, for this reason, quite unreadable, for its talented authors are under the melancholy delusion that half a dozen clinical reports from the waste-paper basket of a psycho-analyst, loosely strung together, are sufficient to give vitality to the corpses which they mistake for characters.

It follows, as it seemed to me then and seems still, that the novelist must have two separate sorts of language in his book. The one, which is uniform and crystallized, is his own style: this he uses for narrative, for such comments as he needs to make, for description, and all such pieces of his book as are not speech. In whatever exciting or depressing or funereal occasions he employs that, he must keep it in the chosen key, he must in this be tranquil and in tune, and not modulate from key to key to suit the current or the coming crisis. He is scarcely more than the man who raises the curtain: he must not pull it up with laughter and alacrity if something humorous is on the way to his readers, nor sigh and sob if hearts are to be wrung. He must not rejoice, in his narrative and comments, with those who rejoice, nor weep with those who weep, any more than he must write his narrative in Irish brogue if a man from Tipperary is about to appear, or in cockney if he is dealing with East London. There must be no patches, even purple ones, in the perfect narrative.

His other style, instead of being simple and uniform, must be as varied and multiform as are the personages in his masterpiece. If two of them talk alike (given they are not intended to be alike), that is a fault in characterization, and a more serious one than if, unintentionally, he made two of them to resemble each other in face and bodily mien. Worse still (but oh, how commonly happening) is it if they all talk alike, and worst of all if they all talk in the style of the author's narrative, for then they become mere dressed-up dolls sitting on the author's knee, while he opens their mouths in turn, and by a clumsy ventriloquism, not altering the tone of his voice, puts his own speech into those inorganic cavities. Instead, the author must have a vocabulary and a phrasing for each of them, and though it is wise of him to write good grammar when he narrates, it is probably a mistake if his characters are all as immaculate as he. We all of us, for instance, split our infinitives in ordinary speech, and though in the mouth of the narrator a split infinitive may (possibly) be an error in grammar, a similar use on the part of one of his speakers is not an error at all. (I drag in this little piece of information for the enlightenment of the tutorial persons who produced the strange volume called

The King's English, and who quote speeches from the books which they pillory, as proof of the author's inability to write grammatically.)

This voracious and indiscriminate reading was hugely enjoyable in itself: I was greedy to know all manners of imaginative visions and, by study, to appreciate them, and I gulped books down with the thirst that cannot be assuaged with sipping, but must swill. But behind that was this insatiable curiosity as to the technique of writing, and even while I was swilling, I would stop suddenly and begin to sip and taste, if something of technical value arrested me, and in particular (to mount the favourite horse again) if some turn of phrase in the mouth of one of the characters suddenly brought to birth something with which every page had really been pregnant. I turned back over the pages, when I came to some such crucial delivery, to find out how this had been subtly prepared, so that, amazing as it might be, it was also, from the point of view of construction, inevitable. In a well-composed book there was no such thing as a surprise for an attentive reader: the climax did not soar unsupported, like a firework, into the air, it climbed on the solid stable rungs of the ladder which, all the time, the author had been quietly erecting.

Impulsive persons (in the book), it is true, must be allowed to do unexpected things, but the unexpected is not a surprise in such a case, but a logical and reasonable demonstration of their impulsiveness. It became a literary crime to me that the authors whom I admired so much should not observe the rules which I had discovered for them : I could not, for instance, forgive George Eliot for daring to tell me, in *The Mill on the Floss*, that Maggie Tulliver, exquisite, delicate, sensitive, fell in love with that bounder Stephen Guest, who wore a diamond ring, and used attar of roses as a " perfume," and whose foppish mind was precisely on a par with his odious personal habits. It was a lie that Maggie Tulliver fell in love with him : she could never have tolerated him. And when, by telling us such a wicked falsehood as that, George Eliot had got her adorable heroine into a tangle that could not be unravelled, she cut the knot which she had wantonly tied, by drowning her in a totally incredible manner. Maggie was out in a boat, you will remember, and though her brother had oars, blocks of machinery, coming down the stream in which was their boat (presumably travelling the same pace, without the oars to help), overtook and overwhelmed them. so I learned that you must not lie about the people you had invented. It was no use to say that you had invented them, and that you had the right to make them behave as you chose. Rather, you were in the witness-box, and, having dared to write a book, were under oath to tell the truth about them.

I took all this trouble in finding out how books were written in order to do it myself. The epoch in which these stories were to be set was now always the same, namely the immediate present, for that was the period that then and ever interested me most. Indeed, just then I was so rapturously immersed in it, that any impression or expression of it went untrimmed into my broth. I had not yet learned any faculty of selection, I was far too impatient to let my materials simmer and soak, and in spite of the strenuousness of my reading, there were only two out of all the errors that can be committed in the writing of fiction into which I never fell.

The first mistake of which I was never guilty was that of writing anything that did not immensely interest me. I wrote in a sunshine of enjoyment, loving the exercise of my craft: never did I return home to my flat after the second session at Niagara with an anticipation of better fun, than when there was ahead of me, reserved and designed for insatiable scribbling, a long, solitary evening. I can still taste the relish of coming in out of a wet November evening, knowing that "they" (the characters in my tale) would be waiting in my sitting-room for me, and presently with "Out" displayed on my door, I would immerse myself and see what they proposed to do. For, indeed, if the book was, in my biassed judgment, going well, it seemed as if the persons I was writing about took charge of their own manœuvres, while I, who held the pen, did little more than record their independent action. Often I would have planned, even with detail, what I meant to do with them, only to find that they had planned and now dictated something else. Of course, it was really my brain that was doing it all, but, so I imagine, some part of it, not quite identical with my conscious self, took control. And when this seemed to be happening, I was careful to distract the more superficial cells. I gave them cigarettes to smoke, occasionally played them a tune on the piano; did anything to divert them so that they should not interfere with what was going on below. And then, incredibly, there would come a ring from the door of my flat, and lo, it was eight o'clock already, and my dinner was arriving from the little Italian restaurant close by, and here was I with the fire half out, unready and unbathed. On these evenings when the mysterious workman was in possession, I took pains not to disturb him, and in this interval for refreshment, forbore to question him about his plans, while I sedulously amused my conscious self, comforting it with a hot bath and a risotto and a bottle of wine, so that, diverted and occupied, it should not meddle. Sometimes it insisted on interfering, and when I got to work again would make itself so importunate that its ally, always sensitive and touchy, would shut up altogether and refuse to make any more plans.

On more fortunate evenings I could quite hold the interfering partner's attention, and with a box of cigarettes and a whisky and soda accessible, he would go on smoking and sipping, engrossed in his carnal pleasures. Swiftly passed those auspicious hours, but at the end the dictating voice ceased, even in the middle of a sentence, and it was long past midnight, and there were a dozen sheets of paper covered with writing on one side of the table, and on the other a half-empty siphon and an ash-tray piled high with stumps, and I between the two symbolic remains, tired and sleepy and wonderfully satisfied. I just arranged the sheets, shuffled off to bed, and slept the perfect dreamlessness of fatigue. After such a night there was a further excitement in the morning, for again and again have I cudgelled my brains as I dressed, in the effort to remember what I had written, and been totally unable to recollect it, so that I would read it over with surprised interest. Often these subconscious scribblings required correction and trimming, for sentences would be unbalanced, and phrases needed the file or called for recasting, but the substance and general outline invariably met with the approval of my conscious self, who realized over his eggs and bacon that he had not and could not have devised the stuff. He might not think very highly of it, but he always passed it on those occasions when he had had nothing to do with it.

I must be pardoned for thus dwelling on this little psychological problem, concerned with creative work, for I think the mechanism concerned has been misunderstood. For everyone who busies himself in mental creative work will allow that he works best *on* something or under certain physical conditions. One man will get up early, when, so he says, his brain is fresh : others will do their thinking when walking about : others, when they are weaving and imagining, will sit in a sort of dreamy quiescence : others will work on tea or tobacco or whisky or possibly opium, for they say that these refreshments stimulate them. But it seems difficult, though one man's meat is another man's poison, to reconcile such various methods of procuring the conditions for creative work as these.

So let us take a totally different hypothesis, which seems to account for the diversity of all these procedures. It looks far more likely that the condition required is one in which the conscious self is quiescent. A night's rest has gratified it in one case, a comfortable arm-chair in another, it is thinking of its cigarette in a third, of its tea in a fourth. But in all these cases, it is occupied and put out of the way, in order that it may not play its monkey-tricks and obtrude itself, when the door of that region of the mind about which we know so little, swings open, and the images of ideas steal forth. The condition in all cases is somewhat similar to hypnosis, in which the conscious self is in abeyance and the subconscious comes to the surface.

This hypothesis fits in with other more transcendental phenomena. The mystic, by meditation from which all things physical are so excluded that he is unconscious of heat or cold or time, sets free the higher powers of his mind, and he " perceives " in supernormal ways. Jacob Boehme, for instance, in order to attain transcendental perception, " ceased from thinking and willing, and made the wheel of his imagination stand still," and it is clear that this state was some sort of self-hypnosis, a stunning and an abeyance of his conscious self, for he tells us that it was accidentally, as he gazed at the bright reflection of sunlight on a copper bowl, that he began to " perceive."

Or to take the other end of the scale in the powers that make up the soul of man, the same thing holds good in physical achievement. Under strong excitement the conscious self is stunned, so that the pain normally arising from a severe physical injury may be quite unperceived, and from somewhere within is let loose a power which enables the muscles and sinews of the body to accomplish feats of which they are normally incapable. But to attain such conditions, one requirement is uniformly essential, the ordinary work-a-day mind has to be diverted : it has to be got out of the way, and whether it is stunned, stimulated, or soothed makes no difference.

For all ideas, all imaginings, from Shakespeare's

down to the smallest scribbler's, come out of some inner sanctuary of the mind, and from behind a veil of impenetrable texture, so that we have no idea whether it is dark within as in the centre of a hive, or radiant with some unimagined light. The conscious mind never sees what goes on there : its functions are to trot about and collect materials, and push its harvestings behind the veil. It will never penetrate beyond : at the most, by insistence and clamour, it seems able to distract and worry that which holds control within, which waits till all is quiet again before it suffers the veil to bulge, and let out some product of its own. Various are its modes of communication with the conscious mind : to Boehme it came through some state of self-hypnosis ; to Stevenson it came in dreams, so that while his body was asleep, as he tells us, he dreamed, for instance, two scenes which are the *clou* of his *Jekyll and Hyde* : to de Quincey it was borne on the wings of drugs, but to all alike it comes, and it comes always, not when the conscious self is to the fore, but when it is asleep or in abeyance or otherwise occupied.

The only other error which I did not commit in those excited days, was the attempt to portray any individual as a leading character in a book.

I have never met, nor shall I ever meet (and if I did I could never learn enough about him), any one person who could possibly bear the burden of being a leading character in any work of fiction, however trivial. Individuals, of course, suggest to the writer the gestures, the appearance, the manners, the flaws and finenesses of character, for, when all is said and done, everybody draws from life, but to suppose that any author could hope for the smallest measure of success if he set himself to reproduce an actual person, in his habit as he lived, to fill a principal place in his romance, is to misunderstand the process of imaginative work altogether. With minor characters, those who are designedly in the background and only incidentally bear on the main conception of a book (which is an idea), it is a totally different question: you may " fill in " with any mild and suitable models. But I early saw and now more fully recognize that the action of a book can only be entrusted to types, composite figures if you will, for in no other way can the presentation be solid.

But since you do not meet types walking about, they must first be internally conceived, and not till then can individuals make their little contributions, and, in fact, the only individual a novelist is ever seriously indebted to is himself.

He draws from himself, from his own unsuspected secret hideousness, his own camouflaged meannesses, and the general objectionableness of his soul a hundred times more often than he draws from anybody else. And if there appear in his delineations some gleam of altruism or generosity, or the difficult heroism of the fireside, you may wager that it has been to his own impulses that he owes his inspiration. For the rest, in his creation of a type which will shoulder the burden of his tale, he owes five per cent. to a man, and four per cent. to a woman, and perhaps six per cent. to a dog. Sex matters nothing to him, a trait from a woman, a manner from a man, a piece of a dog's constancy, and of a cat's aloofness are shredded into the stockpot, with no discrimination of sex or species, in order that there may issue from it, mixed with the overwhelming percentage of the author, typical figures who talk in a consistent and ungrammatical manner. Nothing comes amiss to the author, if only at the end of his shredding and sorcery he can get the strong broth. And so often it turns out to be weak broth. "Let the hen walk through the water once more," as the disappointed *gourmet* said when he tasted the chicken soup.

The moral and the connexion, already I hope

dimly apparent, now emerge. It is because the author draws from himself, that the hours in which his characters seem to take the tiller and steer for themselves comprise the best of his output. It is he, of course, who is really in command all the time, but that region or quality of his brain which knows him most nakedly and intimately is now in charge, and this holds the true compass and the key to such treasures as he possesses. All that he has ever experienced is in that store-house, sorted and arranged, and ready for him if he can only unlock the door and discover his own harvestings. But how difficult that is: in how arbitrary a manner the door swings back and excludes him, and seldom does it stand open for long, and few there are who refuse to write except when the door is open and they have free access to their best. The most of us want to get on with our book, to finish it somehow or nohow, and begin on a new and diverting theme. We let the bright, clever, superficial self take charge, and it turns out something quite neat and readable, but machine-made and unreal. There are cracks and knots in the wood, and we fill up the cracks with putty and put paint over the knots, and apply a coat of varnish to it, and damn our souls. . . .

CHAPTER VII

FRIENDLY and hospitable were those days, and there were a hundred beacons of welcome burning for me on heights or in lowlier places, which I am unorthodox enough (in the way of reminiscences) not to specify. Never a Sunday did I spend in Town, and never did I come back on Monday without a licking of the lips with the sheer enjoyment of it all. Gradually I got more constant in visits to one particular house, which is for ever unique, for I verily believe that there was no house like it before, and there has been no house like it since What gave it its inimitable quality was the personality of its hostess. Park Gate House, Ham Common, was the scene, and the chatelaine was Lady Charles Beresford.

She was in a position no less unique than herself. Once upon a time there had been what we must call a "row," the nature of which can be only faintly indicated. There were four people primarily concerned, two husbands and two wives, of which her husband was one husband, and she one wife, of character never blotched nor blemished, and they were all great friends of a man, who, with his wife, occupied a very prominent position in the London world. When the row occurred, this man, who was always noted for his inexhaustible good-will towards his friends, tried, by a personal interview with Lady Charlie, to smooth over this rough passage, and pointed out what a pity it was to quarrel. But he had rather misunderstood the situation, and he only managed to convey to her the unfortunate impression that his interpretation of the row was an insult to her, and so no doubt it was. She did not pause to consider whether he meant well or not, but ordered him out of the house, and instantly proceeded to write a truthful and candid and voluminous letter to Queen Victoria, telling her all about it with singular directness. Of course, that was not a usual thing to do, rather it was a unique thing to do, but then Lady Charlie was a unique and not a usual woman.

This kind-hearted man, already resenting her order to get out of the house, resented even more this misconstruction of his amiable motives being recounted to the Queen, and he and his friends, who constituted a powerful party, made, not so much an attack on Lady Charlie, as an oblivion of her, a smooth, blank, prodigious wall. So she, with great wisdom, refrained from recalling herself to the oblivious, but raised a regiment of new friends, and, with her back to the prodigious wall, formed a circle which for wit and movement and content and centrality has never been equalled. Instead of behaving like an exile, doomed to wander in bitter homelessness, she settled down most comfortably, and turned the desert into an oasis to which no end of thirsty pilgrims flocked. She never affected to despise the Paradise from which she was an outcast Peri, but was thenceforth blankly unaware that there existed any Eden but her own, and if she came in contact with any of its unfallen inhabitants, she was more unaware of it than ever. For herself, she loved absurdity and originality, she was ignorant, blankly ignorant, of what convention meant and what snobbishness meant, and she was firmly convinced, after many trying and extensive experiences, that the only tolerable mode of life was to be amused. If you were not amused, you were either bored or worried, and she had a great deal that might possibly have worried her if she had succumbed to such a weakness. Women without number had been in love with her husband, but she never. So when he, fascinating and adored and gay and inimitably humorous, seemed to be inflammable also, her heart never suffered. But she had a sense of possession, and a perception of trespass. She disliked all women, except the mature and the plain, and never, if she could help it, saw a girl.

Lady Charlie was at this time on the heights of her amazing and effervescent vitality, and well-embarked on the sea of middle-age which can be so placid to women who have enjoyed enormously and have loved passionately, and have then waved final farewell to the receding coast of youth ; and can be so stormy to those, men and women alike, who have not acquiesced, and will not relinquish their determination to be young in however gaunt and grisly a manner. But she, in some inimitable manner, navigated a sea that was not placid because of her relinquishments and acquiescences, nor yet a sea that was still stormy because she would not acquiesce. Her mind was perennially young, and she was immune from the assaults of temperament : she was as harmless, temperamentally, as a dove, and could, without a moment's pause, be either as wise or as venomous as a serpent. She was often both.

Her diversions and personal appearance, no less than her speech, admirably expressed her. I often went down there on a Saturday morning, in order to have a good long talk from (rather than with) her, before other arrivals, being quite well aware that I was just an ear, which she conceived to be a moderately intelligent one, and one that delighted to have poured into it the inexhaustible torrent of her surprising reflections. Probably she was in the garden, mounted (if no more) on her tricycle, for her doctor had recommended her to take exercise, " and I can't walk, my dear, there's something odd about my knees." Sometimes she trundled herself to the end of the gravel path in the garden, a distance of some hundred yards, but generally she did not get so far, for the tricycle stuck in damp places or on the edge of the lawn, and she dismounted and left it there, for her Pekinese dogs to bark at.

She was shod in very small, high-heeled satin shoes for her exercise, and pale blue and pink were the hues of her habiliment: her hat was a wide umbrella, made of muslin and wires, with large blue convolvuluses trained about it, and she wore a loose gown, suitable for a stout girl of ten, falling straight from the anchorage of her shoulders and fastened fortuitously here and there with large turquoise-headed brooches. There was no pretence about the turquoises: they were enormous plaques of flawless azure, which defied not detection, but deception. "Bon marché," she said, when M. Cambon, the French ambassador, politely admired them, "eight francs each." The same scorn of deception declared itself in her face: a firm eyebrow drawn in charcoal and steeply arched might be the decoration on one side, and she had, as likely as not, forgotten to draw the eyebrow on the other side, or had put on an eyebrow of another species made of an adhesive strip of a sort of fur. Once when she was cruising in the Admiralty yacht in the Mediterranean, a small parcel arrived for her which had burst in the post, and all the eyebrows had fallen out. . . . The powder rose from her face like driven snow if there was a wind, and when she ate an apple (strongly recommended by Dr. Yorke-Davis) a wonderful carmine stained the pale flesh of it. She had puffs and puffs of auburn hair, but no deception there, for how, if that was so, could she have said to me when I played an awkward card at bridge, "Dodo, if you insist on playing that card, I shall take off my hair and throw it at you.". . . The reason why she wore the turquoises and the evening shoes and the eyebrows was quite alien from deception: she wore them in the French spirit, to give her the mask and the confidence of *maquillage*. She saw herself so, and she talked like herself and behaved like herself when she knew that she looked like that. She was forced to have auburn hair and carmine lips in order to say the things she said: they would have been *macabre* otherwise.

And what talk it was: shrewd and penetrating and piffling, defying disentanglement.

"I've read the manuscript you sent me," she said. "Where are my dogs? Blackie, come here at once, and don't make nuptials with Orange among the petunias. I read it in bed last night, and Blackie was lying on my chest, so that when I giggled he fell off. But I wonder if you ought. I'm an old woman, of course, and I never go into the world, and I don't know what's going on. But you mustn't exaggerate: probably you don't, and then so much the worse. And do be on your guard against sentimentality. Sentimentalists are people who want to have the luxury of emotion without paying for it. The turquoise brooch? No, don't bother: they'll find it. Let's have lunch. They will see I've left the tricycle somewhere and find the turquoise. A dreadful day to-morrow! I asked three ambassadors to come down in the afternoon and stop for dinner, and they're all coming. Ambassadors! What's the use of ambassadors when things are in this state? War, my dear, there'll be war between us and France in six months. The French hate us: they hate our levity and our insincerity and our superficiality: all the faults that we attribute to them. Blackie, do not eat pansies: naughty! The French are the most serious and steadfast nation in the world: you will see when war comes. We think they are frivolous, because we can understand nothing but frivolity. Did you go to the opera last night? Tristan: such a bore! And the love-duet! it was time for their golden wedding before they got to the end. The English fleet? There isn't any English fleet: there are a few leaky dinghies which will go to the bottom if they fire a single gun. Ask Charlie if you don't believe me. Yes: Tristan! How marvellous! Why does nobody love like that now? and for heaven's sake let us go in out of this awful sun. It ought to be electric light. Where is Orange? Orange chases the stags in Richmond Park, and I am terrified that one day she will catch one up, and be kicked or bitten to death, or whatever stags do to their enemies. I only have baked apples for lunch; it reminds me of Eden. Is that crab you've got there? Give me a small piece of crab. I will tell Yorke-Davis, I have had crab-apples. Don't be so silly!"

So she would eat some crab, and the telephone bell rang.

"Find out who it is, Nicholas," she said to her butler, "and say 'no.' I cannot bear the telephone. Why should I be at the beck and call of everybody? You must come to Baireuth with me next year. Whenever I travel, something extraordinary happens: either the engine won't go, or the guard commits suicide, or somebody with whom I am not on speaking terms claims my sleeping-berth. Why don't you put the telephone into your flat, a separate one, I mean? Whenever I ring you up, something sepulchral moans at the other end and says it will see, and when it does see, I can't hear. I couldn't live without the telephone. Have you seen Maisie? I am told she has gone into deep mourning over Tim's death like a widow. Of course everybody knew, but she needn't remind them: so silly to dot the i's when the man's dead, and the i's have all been dotted again and again already. But crape, swathed in crape, like a crow, and almost tumbling out of her box last night at the Liebestod. I suppose it reminded her of him. How like the scene in a novel I couldn't read—Hall Caine isn't it, or do I mean Marie Corelli?—where the marriage service is interrupted by a female coming out from behind the organ, and shrieking, " You promised to make an honest woman of me!" Just as if any man could make a woman honest! What an awful sex we are, and how I hate all that sort of thing. Dusé is coming down to-morrow: I hope she will not make a scene with Mrs. Patrick Campbell: aren't they both acting Magda? What a play! A country vicarage invaded by the sweepings of Leicester Square! We must get some fresh blood down here." . . .

A few habitués probably arrived for dinner that night, but it was not till Sunday that the party, this wonderful and inimitable party, grew populous. Always there were weird and curious people among it, and Lady Charlie wondered why she had asked them, and her husband grouped them under the head of Tishbites, " Mina's Tishbites." On one occasion the Ambassadors of France and Italy arrived earlier than she expected or wanted them, and so exclaiming, " They will amuse each other," she retreated to the kitchen-garden until a large consumption of strawberries enabled her to meet them. When she came back her guests, already numerous, were playing bridge and croquet, as if at a club. There were large summer-houses scattered about the garden with one side open to the air, and the others of trellis or match-board: these were completely furnished with chairs and tables and carpets and books, and in summer there was bridge going on in one, and tea in another, and impassioned arguments in a third. Sometimes she played bridge, and even in the middle of a hand, if she heard the sound of piano-playing from inside the house, she would depute a guest to finish the rubber for her, and hurry off to see if it was Paderewski, which it never was. And then the pianist would be told to play the last act of the *Gotterdämmerung* because it made her ill for a fortnight with emotion, and she listened for about two minutes, and scolded Blackie for barking, and then plunged into some obscure and obstetric and confidential conversation.

"She thinks that nobody ever had a baby before," she whispered. "As if everyone wasn't always having babies. I could have a baby to-morrow—ah, isn't that wonderful: that's the Tarnhelm motif, and so Brünnhilde thinks it's somebody else. I always tell Charlie he ought to have a Tarnhelm. Entrancing, my dear, I could listen for ever ! Don't get up, but play the *Meistersinger* all through. What, Nicholas ? Oh, has Madame Dusé come ? Where is Mrs. Patrick Campbell, or the Italian ambassador ? They will talk Italian together. My Italian is purely operatic. ' Nobile sposa ' : that sort of thing, and I can't say that to Dusé."

The day waned, and there was an enormous dinner out in the garden. Sometimes everybody stopped for it, and the table lengthened and lengthened itself, or else nobody stopped but those who were staying the night, and a dozen people sat down to viands for a City banquet. She generally asked more guests to stay than there was room for in the house, and one must sleep in the bath, and another on the sofa in the drawing-room. Sometimes those who were going back to Town stayed very late, with Lady Charlie getting more animated and loquaciously amazing as the hours went by, and well I remember one particular Sunday night, when the latest to leave did not get off till two in the morning, and she sent for some more sandwiches and some beer, and insisted on a quiet game of bridge in one of the shelters. Perhaps there were two rubbers or perhaps there were three, and she found the nightingales very distracting and revoked.

"Just when we were getting on so nicely," she said. "One more rubber: that was so short. I don't know what the time is, and let nobody tell me. People invented watches and then became slaves to them. Frankenstein, wasn't it? What a monster! Hughie, do not look at your watch, but cut. Otherwise you will say you must go to bed in order to be fresh and bright for the City to-morrow. Hughie lends the Bank of England a hundred thousand pounds in the morning, and the Bank pays him back a hundred thousand pounds and one penny in the evening, or is it the other way about? But that is the basis of finance."

She gave a loud shriek.

"What is happening?" she cried. "Haven't we had one moon already to-night, and why is there going to be another? There's something coming up there."

Of course it was the sun, and she hastily rose.

"And me as ill as this," she said. "We must all go to bed at once. Blackie, Orange, my darlings, how bad for you to sit up like this!" And with the flowers in her hat stirring in the breeze of dawn, she devoured a strawberry or a caviare sandwich, and shedding turquoises and handkerchiefs and gloves, she hurried off, with Blackie and Orange circling madly round her across the dew-drenched lawn.

In the winter Park Gate House was shut up, and Lady Charlie came to London for a few months, collecting fresh blood for Ham, and virulently criticizing any Government that might happen to be in power. This year I began to spend winters in high Swiss resorts, for the achievement of the gold badge in skating, and started at Grindelwald. But now, more vivid to me than skating, are certain days, when, if the rink was indisposed, or I was a-weary of the elusive art, I tied my lunch to a toboggan, and went off quite alone for the day. There was a mild descent into the valley along which the stream from the Wetterhorn glacier nosed its way under lids of ice towards the Lake of Thun, gurgling and chafing below them, and, where its course was steeper, shaking itself free, and steaming in the frosty air. Its mist was sneezing-cold to the voyager, and I hurried across the icicled bridge, and drew my toboggan briskly up the hill towards the Scheidegg pass. By now, the Bear Hotel and the clustered village round it had dwindled to the scale of toys, and the spell of solitude was weaving. To right and left were fields glistening with silent snow : in front was a pine-wood, capped and caparisoned with white, against which the foliage was jet-black and the tree trunks glowing orange, and above that rose the northern precipice of the Eiger, too steep for more than a powder of snow to lie on it. There was no human being within sight or hearing : here was the joy of it, and under the blue crystalline dome, and beneath the amber heights, I would feel myself shrunk into an infinitesimal atom. That is the magic of solitude : there is no sense of absorbing it, or filling it with your own impressions, and glorying in it ; the solitude invades and all but annihilates you, and the consciousness of existence in it, a quickened and stimulated minuteness, is all that is left of you. . . . Just below the pine-wood one paused, getting rid of the remains of oneself in full breaths, dwindling and dwindling into the rapture of conscious nothingness. In the desert you can thus lose yourself, or by swimming very far out to sea, but nowhere is the loss so complete as in the whiteness of snow and the immense azure.

The climb up through the pine-wood recalled me, for there was the environment of trees ; a scale asserted itself again. They were big, but not so big, and the toboggan grounding on stumps and excrescences was a clue to identity. But even thus it was wonderfully pleasant to be alive and hot and hungry, and, in the reaction, I would make a cache below a pine-root, of a piece of chocolate, and a cigarette and a ten-centime piece. (Or was that only a function of the spirit of solitude, playing a secret game, and being silly with seriousness?) And noticing that midday was past, I hurried on again, telling myself that if I was going to climb the Jungfrau and Monck and Eiger, I must waste no more time. But then, perhaps, there would be a gentian, bluer than the zenith, which had pushed a spiked bud through the snow and radiantly flowered, and the wonder of it, the sense of the colour shouting of beauty in the whiteness and the solitude, enchained me. The image of Bach improvising some miraculous fugue in a huge empty church came into my mind.

I came back in this January of 1901 to spend a few days with Regie Lister in Paris, where he was second secretary in the British Embassy. He met me at the station with the news that Queen Victoria was dead. I had known, like all the rest of the world, that she was old and that she was ill, but I do not think it had ever soberly occurred to me that she could die. To those who had grown to maturity in her reign, it seemed an incredible and shattering convulsion of nature. The Queen belonged to the same order of bodies as the sun and the moon: she had been on the throne before one's mother was born, and only Beth (equally immortal) could remember her accession; majestic and mysterious permanence was her attribute. One had grown out of childhood, and realized that the head on current coin was that of the Queen (the whole coinage of the realm was hers), and one grew out of boyhood and there was the head of the Queen still, with a new design of head-dress and the face of an old woman, commemorating (was it?) her first Jubilee, but it was still the effigy of the imperishable Queen. Once only had I seen her close and quietly. For one year, towards the end of the eighties, my father had taken a house on Deeside for August, and we were all invited to Balmoral. And the diminutive old lady with the prominent blue eyes that looked very fixedly at you and the really beautiful voice, who was so small and so significant, was the head of everything, the incarnation of stability and security, something cosmic. . . . There was, too, something vividly individual about her, and if, never having seen her before, I had observed her walking into some very unexpected place, like a small restaurant in Soho, I verily believe I should have known her for Queen Victoria: nobody else could possibly be quite like that, nor could she possibly have been anyhow different.

That one minute of personal and private experience other than the sight of her in crowds and ceremonials, contributed to, rather than diminished, the lone dignity in which the Queen was enveloped, and after that day she, in her lameness and her littleness and her sovereignty, became to me, more potently than ever, one of the elemental facts in the world, and it was amazing to see, as Regie Lister and I drove through the streets of Paris on that cold January morning, that the French world, not a bit stunned, was carrying on just as before. Even London, whither I returned in a couple of days, was behaving as usual, and then, at Windsor, where I went for the funeral in St. George's Chapel, I saw the supreme pageant of empire and splendour and simplicity.

She had died at Osborne, and the body was brought across from the Isle of Wight on the *Victoria and Albert*. It passed through the mourning capital, and arrived at the station at Windsor much behind the time, so that there was a very long period of waiting for those in the Chapel. The robed Knights of the Garter were in their stalls, both Houses of Parliament were there, but by some mistake a whole batch of commands to the funeral had miscarried, and a large block of seats in the nave, close to the entrance to the choir, was empty. Then came the drone of drums, and the wailing of fifes, faint and distant, from the station, and you visualized the train from London drawn up there, and the porterage of what it bore. And again the minutes went by and for a while the wailing ceased, and somehow in whispers it became known that one of the horses harnessed to the gun-carriage had shied and tried to bolt, and that the horses were taken out, and bluejackets of her fleet dragged the bier up the steep slope from the station and across the High Street.

Then there was some quiet stir round the west door of the chapel, and though yet nothing could be seen, the black lines of people on either side of the gangway up the nave, rose to their feet. Outside the day was grey, with pale glimpses of sunlight, and now in the middle of the open doors, there appeared, like a shadow across the brightness, something small and square, wavering and swaying as it was carried up the steps outside the chapel. On either side of it were little round blots, and soon, as they mounted to the level of the nave, you perceived that these were the heads of those who bore the coffin. Up the nave she came, with that slow swaying rhythm, and there followed her the King of England and the German Emperor, and the princes who were her sons and sons-in-law, and her nephews and her grandchildren, and on her coffin, when it came to rest, there were laid the sceptre and orb and crown of her royalty. Never had she been so great as now, nor ever her death more incredible than when for the last time all rose as she passed by. The Garter King-of-Arms recited who she was, Queen of Great Britain and Ireland, and Empress of India, and when he had finished he said, "God save the Queen." It might be hundreds of years before that was ever said again, and the whole greatness of her rose to its highest. But higher yet, immeasurably, rose that for which she stood, and its splendour which she had upheld. For the Garter King-of-Arms recited the style and titles of Edward, King of Great Britain and Ireland, and Emperor of India, and when he had finished he cried, "God save the King!" . . . It was over, and by the coffin stood the King of England and the Emperor William II of Germany.

CHAPTER VIII

MANY were the backgrounds of life in front of which, in scenes of security and sense of home, I plied the art of engrossed living, with extraordinary pleasure. I had not the permanent roadstead of marriage, but was anchored to many friends, of whom Regie Lister was the chief, and much at home in many houses, and most of all there was Tremans. If ever I had a sense of bleakness, here or there, I knew that there were special sunlights, where I could go for basking. Words cannot convey to those who do not adultly remember pre-war conditions how secure life felt. There was, of course, the South African War going on, but serious and anxious though it was, the sense of distance dimmed it to the ordinary citizen.

The visit to Baireuth with Lady Charles Beresford, hinted at before, duly took place, and her assertion that when she travelled extraordinary things occurred was fully justified. But even more extraordinary things were in progress at

Baireuth, for Siegfried Wagner, son of the Master, who conducted the *Ring*, was aware that there were more Masters than one, which never had been the case before. For when I asked him if his own opera had been performed again, he answered : " No : I have to wait for recognition : the same thing happened to my father." There was a revelation in that simple sentence : he knew that his father had a son, whereas, two years before, no such blasphemy had ever penetrated into Wahnfried. Then the son had a father, and the widow had had a husband, but nothing else was known about them ; their glory was but that of the moon which owes all its light to the central luminary.

The most buxom of the Rhine-maidens, she who swung the highest, and sang the heartiest, fell in love with Lord Charles Beresford at first sight, and managed to leave little notes on his cane-bottomed stall, of an inconceivable amorousness, and written in German, which, as he was unacquainted with the language, must be interpreted. Lady Charlie used to hurry to her seat, " pinch " the note that was intended for him, and (knowing German perfectly) greedily to devour it. He followed with a broad grin, and said, " Hullo, Mina ; been reading my private correspondence again ? What does my girl say ? Translate it to me, and don't leave out the warmer passages. You listen, Dodo; when you're over fifty you won't find that anyone writes to you like that. Yes: she's the one who begins on the left of the stage, and goes full speed ahead like a boat in a high sea. Well-nourished woman, and comes from Palestine, I should think. She called me her little partridge yesterday. Spit it out, Mina: perhaps I'll be a pheasant to-day."

All this, though diverting, smudged the traditional sacredness: the *Dämmerung*, of which I have already spoken, had certainly begun. Munich, for instance, was spreading its tail like a peacock, owing to the success of its last season's Wagner performances, and Mrs. Craigie, who was of our party, said in a moment of strong moral courage that Wotan was a bore, and emboldened by these heresies, Mr. George Moore framed the impious theory that *Parsifal* was composed by an organist in collaboration with a choir-boy. But while despising and despairing of him, one perceived what he meant. It was not that I agreed with him in the remotest manner, but I recognized that if you happened to hold that disagreeable point of view, there was something to be said for it, and Mr. Moore said it. Surely no one had ever such a genius as he for detecting flesh where you had imagined spirit, for picking at the splendid until he revealed below it the sordid. In that evocative flash (as Mr. Hewlett might say) one saw it all, the organist, nodding to the choir-boy to pull out the *vox humana*, and the light from a stained glass window falling on their faces. The fact, of course, was that the glamour was for me a little fading from Baireuth, or else we should not have paid so much heed to what Mr. Moore said about music.

But the faculty of finding glamour will not permit those who possess it to inhibit its functions; until the world quite fades into the light of common day the glamorist will always find enchanted places, and for me the glamour which had grown pale at Baireuth was beginning to glow at Tremans. There the adjustment of the new relationship between my mother and sister had been effected and established, and now the years up to the summer of 1906 seemed to pass for its inhabitants like some long, tranquil and yet busy afternoon hour, sunny and softly mellow. There was Beth, already over eighty, ailing but seldom, and for ever actively trotting about the house and rummaging in our wardrobes, whenever Arthur or Hugh or I came home, to find linen and socks which needed mending, and carrying off all such to her room, where, sitting in the rocking-chair in which she had soothed two infant generations to sleep, she darned and patched. There she sat, bright-eyed and eager for visits from her children, and if Hugh was not to be found, it was because he was having a crack with Beth, or if Beth was not to be found, it was because she was sitting with Maggie in the shelter in the orchard ; while for an hour before dressing-time in the evening, there was only one place in which to look for my mother, for she was reading aloud to Beth. Dickens was the favourite author, and to see Beth laughing over the Kenwigses was a lesson in glee.

Then there was Maggie, better in health than she had been for ten years, directing the affairs of the St. Paul's Society, and, no less, those of hens and cats and cinnamon turkeys, and ever so surely and solidly proceeding with her philosophy. More often than not Miss Gourlay or Miss Gladys Bevan, those two most devoted friends, would be with her, giving themselves to her with the completeness with which Lucy Tait was my mother's. . . .

And finally and firstly there was she, entering on

the period of her sixties, alert for all kinds of travel. The years of looking back, of regret, of loss and emptiness which had succeeded my father's death, had passed like some cold wind, which had delayed but not damaged the fruit which the mellow years now ripened. She hated certain physical disabilities, curtailments of energy, that were incident to age, and made endless plans for dieting and for mapping out the hours in a secret book, and therein recorded dismal failures, and set to work again. Her eyes troubled her sometimes, but with no serious threatening, and if on a damp morning she was rather rheumatic, she still left all her occupations on the suggestion of a walk, prefacing it with, "If you don't mind a totter with a tortoise." But when such disabilities assailed, they were but the beating of waves on a strong coast, and above it, flaming more lucently than ever, was the lighthouse of her soul. Not one beam of its illumination was quenched now: it had been darkened only by some external clouding of its lenses. Privately and confidentially she might admit certain worries, but the measure of her light and her strength was that when friends or sons were with her she utterly refused to acknowledge them. She was not at home to them; they had come to the wrong house, or, at the most, they might wait by the back-door, well out of sight. The gods had given her the temperament of flame and imperishable youth of mind, always vastly interested and keenly critical, and a marvellous gift of right phrasing. Of one acquaintance with a childish and immature outlook she would announce, " She wants a bottle, but she must have beef "; of another, " Her perplexity is as to whether God can be trusted "; of another (who had certainly bored her with the efficient but soulless details of some scheme), " Oh, what water for the thirsty of the accurate and the intricate."

But to Lucy Tait, the friend of her heart, she confided all that secretly worried her: she spoke to her as if to herself, admitting the mutterings of fear and flesh on which her courage imposed silence towards others, and she records in her diary, with impatient amusement at herself, the following tragic scene. " Last night," she says, " something prompted me to ask Lucy whether she considered me a grumbler. She said very promptly, ' Yes.' I asked, ' Let 20 be the maximum grumbler, what mark do you give me?' and she answered ' 15.' . . . There is all told. She tried to water it down, but it was a facer. Let me think what she means:

I think it is detailed and continual comparing of 'then' and 'now,' and my mentioning discomforts and disagreeable conditions and dwelling on them. I see only one way—abandon all expressions of everything of the kind, and of unfavourable small criticisms. Under cover of this, the change, please God, may be made. Content and joy for grumbling and sadness, the garment of Praise for the Spirit of Heaviness. . . . Maggie's kind of illness and condition all works in into this grumbling, which Lucy finds in me. I think I had better not talk to her about it at all and have no confidant. Be as one who goes to live in a French family. Be glad not to be natural till the new nature is born in me. Have advancing years and changed and narrowed circumstances produced in me a smaller range, and a greater dislike to be bothered? As age draws on and death comes nearer, am I living more in the real existence, or less? Oh, do let me think."

My mother made this entry when a shadow, perhaps the darkest of all that ever crossed her path, was beginning to fall. She just alludes to it in " Maggie's kind of illness," which belongs to a later date. . . . But the whole entry is marvellously characteristic of her. She had no doubt indulged herself to Lucy Tait in what she so magnificently concealed from the rest of us, and had clearly, in fact, been grumbling. Then, gloriously, it is a facer to her to know that the friend was perfectly aware of this and quite candid, so instantly my mother pounces on herself, all claws and teeth, to tear out this prodigious hideousness from her nature. Without a hint of resentment at the judgment, she searches herself to see what it comes from, with all that passion for analysis which made human motives and weaknesses so interesting to her. She must not permit herself a single further grumble : dead silence, and under cover of that wait for the birth of a better nature. . . . For it never struck her, then or at any other time, that, from the days when she studied French cathedrals in order to please my father, her life had been spent in self-surrender to those she loved. But then she analysed herself always from the standpoint of infinite love, and admitted no measure of that which she ought to be but the immeasurable.

She began in those years to care about the country in itself, for it was associated with the health which had returned to Maggie and the peace that had come to her, and, even if it had been possible, she would not now have chosen to settle in London. There was always the little house in Barton Street to which she could go, but she was seldom there for long, and when, presently, that was given up, she had a home with Archbishop Davidson and his wife in the old scenes of Lambeth. She still loved the sense of affairs swiftly and ardently a-stir round her, and nothing of her passion for live people had abated, but, with the gentle shower of the years falling on her, she began —just a little—to find a strain in the continuance and multiplicity of such stir, and preferred to have intimates, such as her sister-in-law, Mrs. Henry Sidgwick, Adeline Duchess of Bedford, and her sister, Lady Henry Somerset, with her at Tremans, where there was leisure to enjoy them, and the household there was seldom confined to itself.

She had certain early hours set apart for devotions and meditation, and she had a considerable correspondence, which daily took her some time, but that was immensely interrupted (even when the rest of the family were busy, and didn't imperatively want her that minute) with entertaining Joey, an extremely vicious green parrot, whose cage stood at her elbow as she wrote, and who blindly adored her. Joey would be let out and allowed to walk up her arm and perch on her shoulder, and laugh hoarsely into her ear. She gave him attractive, hard objects, empty reels of cotton and small, stiff, cardboard boxes, to play with, his method of play being to tear them into small shreds. Then Joey went for a walk on the floor, ready to run at anyone who came into the room, insane with rage that he and his beloved should be intruded on. Luckily there was a stand of walking-sticks near the door, and the intruder was wont to snatch one up, and hold the end of it out to Joey, who could not resist perching on it, and then you could wipe him off into his cage and shut the door. There was a shrill penny-whistle for his amusement, and my mother blew on it, and Joey a-quiver with musical ecstasy whistled selections from his one tune, "Pop goes the Weasel." Beth did not like Joey; she said he was not "kind and loving," which but faintly expressed his satanic nature, but whoever came in, Joey would be wiped into his cage, and the unfinished letter put aside, or the account-book bundled back into the Italian cabinet, and there she was, interminably ready for anyone who wanted her to stroll and talk and sit in the garden, or, if the panes streamed and rattled, to sit over the fire and still talk.

Sometimes she tried to shake herself up into an interest in politics, national affairs, and burning questions of the day, but no question concerning collective interests and the affairs of masses burned so bright for her as those of individuals, and it was concerning individuals that the affairs of Horsted-Keynes, as a perfectly placid little community, were a growing occupation to her. An organist, a school-mistress, a vicar, a monthly nurse, a farmer's boy, were brisk and tidal waters to her, though so short a time before she had found Winchester so unspeakable a stagnation. But the change was in herself : she would have gloried in " the close and the county and the military " now, for the fresh tide was sweeping in from the sea with sparkle and foam and the first rosiness of sunset.

And, presently, the moment she had attained the requisite years, she inimitably conceived an " Association for women over sixty-five," subtitularly headed " The League for the Utilization of Waste Products." The Waste Products must put aside certain hours for their spiritual profit, and, for their physical, must be two hours a day in the open air and eight hours in bed. Then, having done their best for their bodies and their spirits, they might do precisely as they liked for the rest of their time. She records the enrolment of one member (Lucy was not eligible on account of youth), and there are unmistakable marks of

MOTHER

Joey's beak on the note-book in which the affairs of the League are thus set forth.

Meantime, during these years, her sons were getting on with their businesses. Arthur had left Eton, and was officially employed on editing, with the assistance of Lord Esher, the stupendous mass of Queen Victoria's correspondence, and presently with loaded trunks moved to Cambridge, where he became Fellow of Magdalene College, Stuart Donaldson, an old Eton colleague, being Master. Magdalene was then hardly a college at all; there were not more than thirty undergraduates, but from the moment of the application of these combined energies, it began to expand and voluminously flourish, growing in a few years to the position and prestige of an important college.

And as if all this was but a mild canter for his projection, he brought out books of such delicate and finished workmanship as *From a College Window* and the *Upton Letters*. The wonder of it was, that whereas anyone would imagine that for such detached and reflective work leisure and immunity from all practical roughnesses was necessary, he passed from College meetings and mid-Victorian politics, as with a dive, into those fragrant seclusions, or, with the ink still wet on his pen, and dispensing with an architect, drew plans for a house at Cambridge, which flowered into an admirable residence. Simultaneously, so it seemed, he would be shooting in Scotland, playing bezique with my mother at Tremans, and bemoaning the fact that he had never a minute to himself. " It's sickening, it's infernal, the grind of it all," he said. " Ha ! double bezique. Don't let us have prayers to-night. Or, if you must, Fred shall play the hymn on the organ and I will play obligato parts on the piano ! . . ." And Hugh would notice that Lucy had fallen asleep, while still holding up the evening paper, and made a mysterious scratching sound on the underside, which caused her to start into consciousness and fling the paper wildly from her. Maggie, teaching Taffy his tricks, shouted with laughter, and Taffy, unobserved, put out a large pink tongue, and stealthily swallowed the portion of biscuit for which he ought to have sneezed. " Lucy, you *weren't* asleep," she said. " I swear you weren't asleep." And Beth, on her way down to supper, had to pop in to see what we were all laughing about.

Then there was Hugh ; he had gone to the House of the Resurrection at Mirfield, and there for a time he was intensely happy. Then he began to wonder if this was his real place, and soon he ceased to wonder, for he heard in the stillness of his soul the command for its further adventure. He wrote at that time his first book, *The Light Invisible*, a collection of short stories strung together on the personality of an old Catholic priest, and set in the scene of the house and garden at Tremans. They showed clearly enough how strongly Rome beckoned, and their publication, while he was still in Anglican orders, was somewhat anomalous, though for the sake of a faintly veiled anonymity he called himself " Robert Benson." Subsequently he grew to dislike the book, but there are many who think that, artistically, it is the best he ever wrote, and their reasons for thinking this are precisely the same as those for which Hugh disliked it. For as soon as he had made up his mind that he was going over to Rome, he wrote nothing which did not unmistakably show its propagandist purpose: on the pictures and problems he presented, on the complications and characters and solutions, there is painted the undeviating finger and guidance of Catholicism, and the absence of this in *The Light Invisible* was, to him, its mortal defect: it spoke indifferently and neutrally. But just for that reason, apart from its finished workmanship, others regard it as his best work: it did not preach, it only presented.

From the first he had taken my mother into his confidence : he had told her that he felt he might have to leave the Anglican Church, he told her when the possibility was becoming a probability, and when the probability became a certainty. At no stage of his pilgrimage did he leave her in ignorance of his whereabouts. She, on her side, merited this full confidence, for never once, seeing that the matter concerned only his conscience, his conviction of the dealings of God with his soul, did she attempt to bring any counter-influence to bear : she only wanted to understand, and so she watched and prayed. So deep and so true to her was this knowledge that he was following what he was convinced was guidance, that she never felt the smallest touch of real, authentic regret, for that would have implied that she wished his development other than it was, and this she could not wish, since she believed that all the best of him, as far as he knew it (and nobody else could know it), was acting in accordance with the Divine Will. That was sufficient for her.

Hugh was at Tremans often and long after he left Mirfield, and before he was received into the Roman Communion was gaily posting along with that admirable novel, *By What Authority ?*

But already the propagandist as well as the novelist was busy, a thorn to Anglican noses in the rose he presented. There was the hint in all Hugh's stories from this time forward of rubbing the new Church in and treading on the toes of the old. In one hand he held a humorous and busy pen, in the other, skilfully concealed behind his back, a bottle of the strongest, the most healing R.C. liniment. Sooner or later (usually sooner) he, by some dexterous sleight of hand, laid the pen down, and pouring the liniment out with one hand, rubbed it in with the other.

He had all the violence of a 'vert (per- or con- according to taste), and, as if in the discharge of a duty, he used an incessant pea-shooter on the faces of the bishops and elders of the flock he had left. To argue with Hugh on religious topics, always introduced by him with challenges and defiance, was like playing Rugby football under rules framed by himself. He might collar (so ran the rules) any of the opposing side, and kick their shins and hustle them, and rub their faces in the mud, and stamp upon them, but his opponents must do nothing of the sort: if they did, it was a " foul." If you collared a dogma or a bull on his side, Hugh wore a pained expression and said, " Please don't talk like that: you hurt me when you talk like that"; and then, slipping out, he slapped and pommelled the clergy of the heretic persuasion. When things got too hot, my mother would quote Mrs. Vincy in *Middlemarch*, and say, "Dear me, how pleasant it is to hear young people talk!" and her young people then, with temporary reconciliation, fell on her for her flippancy. . . .

In the house at Tremans was a small room, licensed as a chapel for the celebration of the Eucharist, and now, when, within a year of his "version," Hugh was in priest's orders in the other Church, it became impossible for him to stay with my mother, unless he said daily mass, he (more Rugby football) collared this room. He had, of course, to make some little changes: he procured plaster casts of the Blessed Virgin and a few saints, and grabbing Maggie's box of oil-paints, he spent a perfectly happy morning in tinting their faces, and giving them robes of celestial brightness. There was still a little paint left in some of the tubes when that was done, so he used it on the windows, and made radiant effigies of more saints in their leaded panes. The altar was a large black oak chest with, luckily, two shelves within, and so Hugh allowed the paraphernalia of the Anglican use to occupy one, but took the other for his own. Sometimes he would meet Beth on the stairs, carrying up fresh linen, and he would give her a word of warning, "Now, Beth, don't mix their things up with mine. Pray-a-be careful!" He always brought down some boy to serve him, and in the morning the loud Anglican hymn from family prayers below went on simultaneously with his office.

There were other offices as well, tierces and quarts and quints (I do not profess to give their names accurately), and one morning Hugh and I were playing croquet on the lawn below the window of the chapel, in that mingled spirit of suspicion, passion, and vengeance which accompanies and illuminates all serious croquet. At a crucial point, with a disembodied "rover" prowling about, Hugh suddenly looked at his watch: "Oh, blow it, I must go and say my prayers," he said, and hurried within. From the open window above there came a rapid and confused murmur, and soon, wonderfully soon, Hugh scurried out again and looked balefully at the balls. "I'm sure that ball wasn't there," he said. "Fred, do you promise you haven't moved it?" . . . so little fraternal trust had quints produced. . . .

But first, soon after he had been received, he went off to Rome for an audience with Leo XIII. My mother speeded him to the boat-train at Victoria, alone, as she thought, but even as she ceased waving to him, as the train went out of the station, she felt a hand take hers, and found Bishop Wilkinson of St. Andrews, a very old friend of hers and of my father's, standing with her. He had learned when Hugh was leaving, and that my mother was seeing him off, and with a supreme and comprehending delicacy had left her to make her uninterrupted farewells. But he guessed what Hugh's departure symbolized to her, with the memories of my father so inevitably close to her, and so here he was. " Hugh is in God's hands," he said.

CHAPTER IX

THERE is a Greek legend which, like all things Greek, is drawn from the essence and not the mere accidents of life. A pair of hapless lovers, Halcyone and Ceyx, having offended the high gods, were turned into birds, Halcyons, and, like Paolo and Francesca, were condemned to haunt for ever the empty air. But the compassion inherent in Greek myth, the humanity which has pity on weakness, could not leave them thus perilously and eternally wandering. So every year at the time of the winter solstice a remission for mating-time was granted them, and they built a floating nest on the sea, and reared their young. For that period the waters of the Ægean were calm, no wind vexed its azure. Boreas held his breath and the south wind folded his wings, while the nest of the Halcyons floated on the tranquil tide, and these days were known as the Halcyon days. For the rest of the year there was no peace for the poor Halcyons; they were driven from coast to coast, and on land the cunning of man pursued them, and on the sea the white-capped foam of waves. But when the Halcyon days came round, they built in security on the wine-dark sea. . . . Ornithology has identified the Kingfisher with the Halcyon, but it was clearly of some sea-bird, the tern perhaps, that the legend tells, though, as far as I know, no bird mates in mid-winter, nor makes a floating nest on the sea. But it is not the species that matters, it is the spirit of the legend that gives it life.

Everyone who has lived and sinned against the high gods can apply the legend. Sorrow and regret and fears and fleeing are a universal heritage, but to all there sometimes comes that season of calm weather, even in the midst of their winter, and the nest floats on a quiet sea, and the bitter winds are still, and all the scurryings and disturbances of the past are dead, and no clouds threaten the clear shining. . . .

Sometimes a little group of persons, though widely differing in age and taste and temperament, arrives at such a solstice together, and it was so with the family whose history I am recording. For nearly two years the five of us, my mother, three brothers, and a sister, with Beth and Lucy, those inseparable allies of us all, both welded into the family heart, basked in Halcyon days. Though I can speak authoritatively for no one but myself, I think we really liked each other, though sharply disagreeing, better than anybody, and though our lives lay widely apart, we were strongly and fundamentally united. We three sons, as already has been recorded, were busy and prosperous in foregrounds of work and diversion, but to us all the sense of "home" resided behind in the old red-brick house at the end of the avenue of pines, and in the serenity and well-being that dwelt there. Never had my mother been so free, as in those years, from fear, that ghostly enemy of hers, whom she was always trying to throttle, and who kept raising spectres for her, the grimness and unreality of which were truly surprising even to herself. They were always small things, a minor ailment of one of her flock, or some little risk that another was running, which evoked these bogeys: when great trouble threatened, and when intense anxiety was justified, her fears vanished like a frosty breath in the presence of that which made the sunlight of life to her, namely her unreserved acceptance, more and more unclouded as the years went on, of the will of God. For of her it is literally true to say, that the intenser the anxiety, the more shattering the blow, the more completely the mists dispersed, leaving her bathed in the radiance of her faith. There was no such attitude possible to her as resignation or folded hands when trouble was heaviest : for these great dealings she had nothing but clear welcome for what God was sending, and hands uplifted not in prayer but in praise. . . .

But just now, in these two years of Halcyon weather, she neither evoked her little spectres, nor must call on her faith to meet trouble : she found, too, great happiness in the knowledge that the very intimate personal relationship in which she stood to each of her children was quite unaffected by any divergence of opinion, between her and them, as to their modes and manners of life, and their employment of their energies. She would, for instance, have delighted in Arthur's becoming Head Master of Eton, and she was unfeignedly sorry when he refused to stand for it, on the resignation of Dr. Warre, though it had been clearly indicated that if he did he would be elected. But he chose not to—and there it was, and his decision did not depress by the downiest feather's weight the steady balance of his relationship to her, any more than did Hugh's secession to Rome, or (in a minor way) the fact that it was becoming common knowledge between her and me that she found the sort of book that I was writing now quite intolerable, though none of us yet had written anything that gave her any sense of personal pride. She thought, as far as I can guess, that it was wonderfully clever of us all to write so many books, and she had a home for them all—such a spacious home was it growing—in the bookcase in her sitting-room. There was an Arthur-shelf, and a Hugh-shelf, and a Fred-shelf, and because these propagating volumes were her sons', she exercised a savage guardianship over them, and would never lend her copies. But they didn't give her joy, because she did not agree with the standpoint from which any of them was written. Some struck her as too quietist for the world, and some too worldly for her own quietism: some were propagandist of beliefs she did not share, and some were sentimental, and some were crude, and I feel convinced that she never read twice anything that any of us had written, nor indeed would have read much of it all once, if it had not been we who had written it. She liked "bits" in most volumes of this library, but not one spark of inspiration, not one crumb of the bread of life, did she find in any of them.

On the other hand, I don't think she ever found

inspiration or reality in any books, though she read a good deal. She was not a reader at all in the sense that she ever sought for or found a new world in books. For what she loved to the exclusion of everything else, apart from her spiritual life, was human beings themselves, not imagined ones but real ones, the silly, clever, stupid, talented, spirited, materialistic people who made life so extraordinarily interesting. She adored knowing about the oddities and normalities of real people, their frivolities and splendours, their faiths and their blindnesses, their littlenesses and their magnificences. These were her constant preoccupations: she wanted to learn all about them, why they did this, and why, oh! exactly why, they didn't do that, and if they didn't know, she could probably tell them. . . . And out of these preoccupations sprang her passion which was friendship, and on her friends she poured the gold of her nature, making Danae of them all. But the better she loved, the more critical she became: it was just because her friends were all the world to her, that she longed for their perfecting, for the best of them. She sought God in them no less than in her own devotions, and seeking, she always found, and when she knocked at a heart, it was the best of her friend

MOTHER

that pulled itself together and answered the summons of her love, and so it was, in the old stock phrase, that everyone felt the better for knowing her.

There was her charm and her wit as well, but chiefly it was this rummaging of hers in the rag-bag of your mind, this picking out of anything pleasant, this holding of it up to you, saying, "There! Isn't that nice of you?" which produced the sense of betterment. But this delicious optimism did not inhibit her critical faculty. Whatever she found that was nice could be made nicer yet: whatever was not nice she passed by quickly, not looking. And the very fact that she did that made you ask her to turn back again, and flash the light on to it, till like a moth it fluttered out of its darkness towards this analytical, critical, abounding love. . . . I linger on this aspect of her, because it was that which made the spirit of Tremans, and pervaded the house like the scent of the wood-smoke and the wallflowers below the windows. No one who ever came there escaped the fragrance of it in those Halcyon days. And when the Halcyon days were done, that flame of hers became, more wonderfully yet, the steady light above the storm of perilous seas and the blinding drift.

It was in the late summer of 1906 that the little cloud arose from the sea, which no one noticed at first but my mother. Maggie had been rather over-weighted with work and the sultry weather, and was suffering from some such little gloom as at times overshadow the most equable. My mother assumed that it was earned and creditable fatigue which had produced this, but on talking it over with Maggie, she found that she was secretly and instinctively longing for the old relationship between them, when my mother protected and she was a child and an invalid. Maggie wanted, now when she flourished in health and vigour amazingly restored, to go back to the old sheltered days. . . . Next morning, my mother, puzzled, but not yet anxious, went in to see her as she breakfasted in her own room, and found Maggie in the grip of some fierce depression. She asked what was the matter, and Maggie said, "Oh, I am killing it!" It was then that she knew that the first skirmish of a mortal struggle had begun.

From that day, until the crash and the crisis came, when again my mother swept all the mists aside, and rose to meet the will of God, I do not think she passed a day when she was not ridden by the spectre of Fear. In the world she had a face too gay to admit the suspicion of bravery, but she was inwardly beleaguered and beset with presage and insecurity. Just that one utterance that Maggie was " killing something," soaked deep into those undiscerned regions where the inmost self dwells, and day after day she cried out, in her private diary, to be delivered from Fear, always that. . . . There was as yet no justified reason for her fear: Maggie came back to a serene and active level, but somehow, to the prescience of my mother's mind, the firm ground was quaking.

By Christmas, the little cloud was menacingly visible. After one talk with my mother, in which Maggie spoke of a dread, a darkness, she told nobody about this sense of interior tumult by which she would not permit herself to be frightened, but the effort to preserve the stability of courage became apparent. She would not allow herself to cower before the approach of this stormy wind and tempest which was driving up: she occupied herself with all that she had found so wholesomely absorbing in the Halcyon days. She saw much of her friends, and with a superb self-control finished her book, *The Venture of a Rational Faith*, rewriting it for the second time, but bitterly she knew what she called " these times of just holding on." Sometimes the menace stood away from her, but it threatened again not with the lightened pressure of a condition that was on the mend, but with a deeper grip. She still set her mind on all things external to herself, and with an eager hope of recovering quietude and balance through change of scene she went down to Cornwall for a month. With yearning hands she drew to herself, as a cloak against the storm that now impended, the magic of the early southern spring, clinging to the beauty of sea and land and the joyful creatures of God, always adorable to her : " the colours of the foam and the freshness, and the shells and the sand ! " And she wrote of " this Cornish garden with palms and citrons and fruiting bananas and tree-ferns . . . and birds that come round and chide you, if you haven't brought cake," or " the terraces where you can look down on the back of a sea-gull, and see his yellow webbed feet paddling through the water." Desperately she clung to all wholesome and lovely things, for round her the cloud thickened, and she acknowledged now the blackness of its terror. She would still insist that there " was really nothing the matter beyond strain and fatigue and general depression," promising that she *would* be happy again, and blaming herself for this present eclipse. But it was a hope she clung to, not a fact, a floating spar that drifted away from the land into deep water.

Maggie drifted out, still holding this spar, on the dark tide, not yet submerged, but knowing the depth of it, and its swiftness. She came to see me in Oakley Street after she got back from Cornwall, and spoke of terrible depression, quietly and serenely, as a brave woman would speak of some mortal disease. "I wanted to see you again first," she said, and when she had gone, I began to wonder what "first" meant. Why had she said "first"? . . . And then she went back to Tremans, and recorded in some letter to me how well Beth was, and how sweet the place. There were bantams and little cats, and her collie hysterically welcoming her, and the pink cherry was a-bloom. My mother and Lucy, who had been away, returned, and then suddenly everything got terrifyingly worse. She slept ill, the world assumed to her an evil and phantasmal aspect, with the spirits of dreadful beasts and demons lurking behind mask-faces of men and women. One morning, my mother telegraphed for her old friend, Dr. Ross Todd, to come as soon as he could. All that day Maggie was very quiet and quite self-controlled, so that my mother had not sent for any of her sons, thinking that perhaps she was disquieting herself in vain. For Maggie still held on; she sat out in the garden shelter, she read, she even made some little plans for the future. But as, resting in her room before dinner, she talked to a friend, the imminence of what was coming reached her, and she quoted:

> " But if I stoop
> Into a dark tremendous sea of cloud,
> It is but for a time." . . .

And then the train that brought guests down from London in the evening went by the bottom of the fields, and presently Dr. Ross Todd arrived, and God knows what might otherwise have happened. He saw her at once, and persuaded her to act normally, and dress for dinner and come down, and he promised her to defend both her and others from herself. Before dinner was over the crash came; violent homicidal mania took possession of her.

At that moment, tragic and shattering beyond all contemplation, my mother shook off all the fears that for the last six months had so closely beset her. More than the worst possible of the imaginings she had shuddered to picture to herself was there raging, but for her there was neither shuddering nor fear any more, but she knelt to receive God's ordinance, and then stood firm and upright in the presence of His will. While human effort of any sort might possibly avail, while prayer might obtain the benefit which was now denied, she had watched and prayed that the cup might pass from her beloved and from her. And now she took the cup and drank of it in faith. All that then immediately happened was lit by that burning flame of her acceptance. Next day in London I got a letter from her saying, " We are in very deep waters "; she wanted us all to come. We all met there, and found my mother perfectly tranquil and without any sense of outrage. Her fears had at the worst pictured for Maggie some melancholia, and in this infinitely greater tragedy, she was infinitely great, and in the dark waters she saw the wonders of God in the deep. All the firmness and stability had returned to the sands which had so desperately quaked: she trod them now without sinking an inch into them.

There was a private home for the insane not many miles off, at Burgess Hill, and there, on the advice of Dr. Savage, Maggie was moved. A few days afterwards, I went to see her there, and perceived what gulf of stormy water lay between us. It was unbridgeable and unswimmable, and she stood on the other side of it. It was still she, but you could not reach her. She was there still, but so far off, even when hands were clasped and, with a sudden clearing, momentary as the flashed signal of her smile, she asked if I had come to take her home.

Soon the fierceness of that first seizure abated, and reports and interviews were so favourable that we were encouraged to hope that in a few months she would have recovered. She came much nearer: her distress and confusion were no longer an impassable waste, but more like some mist which surrounded her, dense sometimes, but at other times almost completely clearing. One could realize that her condition was some physical derangement, some imperfect functioning and no more, akin to the want of control in thought which accompanies drowsiness. And then she got much worse.

All this my mother bore without any shrinking of the spirit, and there was more to come. My brother Arthur, already over-worked with his unsparing demands on himself, and shocked and shaken with the calamity, fell into miserable depressions. It was as if some outlying cloud from the tempest which had engulfed Maggie had driven in through the wide door of his distress and sympathy, and for two years weariness and dismal misery lay thick about him. And all the time the flame of my mother's faith burned undimmed, and steadfastly she looked on the face of Christ in praise and adoration. . . .

CHAPTER X

THE yeast of Italy, implanted years before on a visit to Capri, had begun to rise and bubble in me. It was not what you did in Italy, what you ate and drank and heard and looked at and walked on or swam in, that made Italy so adorable : all these were delectable because you did them in Italy. And yet there were places in Italy, and those among the most renowned, which were just themselves, and no more Italian than they were Russian or Swedish. Venice was emphatically one of these, and though every year now I spent several weeks with that dearest of friends, Helen, Countess of Radnor, in her flat in the Palazzo da Mula, I counted that not as being in Italy, but as being in Venice. Venice geographically is in Italy, but that is accidental.

Venice has her own spell, one that cannot take effect until you have ceased to be a tourist there. You must drown your Baedeker in the Bacino, as Prospero (for opposite reasons) drowned his book, before it can work, and instead of surging about in a gondola from church to gallery, and gallery to church, you must learn to stroll slowly through narrow *calli* in order to soak. It is not forbidden to look at a Tintoret, or to visit San Marco (indeed, I think the true Venetian goes to San Marco every day), but you must sit down in front of the particular picture you wish to see, and when you have seen it, you must not behave like a tourist, and look at other pictures, but go away again. Or, if you sit in San Marco, you must not look fixedly or intelligently or with any desire to learn anything at reredos or mosaic or marble column. You must sit and soak like a frog in a pool, gazing batrachianly about you, and then, without registering any impression, go forth and lose your way in the Merceria, forbearing, above all, to ask where you are, or how you are to get home. Indeed, you had better not get home, but, instead, ensconce yourself in some exiguous eating-house, and call for a *frittura* or a *risotto*, or even for *frutta di mare* (to be eaten, but not to be examined too closely), and however badly you talk Italian, and however well the waiter talks English, never permit yourself to drop into your native tongue If you want something for which you do not know the Italian equivalent, make shift without it.

Then, heavy with food and the afternoon drowsiness, you may slink home, skirting your way in strips of shadow, and avoiding short cuts across open piazzas, and doze on your bed in a chamber darkened by drawn *veneziani*, until the breeze begins to steal up from the sea across the lagoon and drip in through the green slats of your shutters. The torrid, windless heat of early afternoon will have passed in dusk and dozing, and another day begins at tea-time. Often thus in the coolness of early evening have I gone out with my hostess in her gondola across the lagoon, and in the enchantment of sunset, Venice, clustering round the central point of the great campanile in the Piazza, lay like an opal on the edge of the waters, pale pink, pale yellow, pale blue, all clouded lights and smouldering iridescence. Or, lingering later yet, we would take with us a basket of cold viands, and tying up to some grey-headed *palo* that marked the channel, see the deep dusk gather, and watch the fading of the western fires. The night comes on swiftly in these southern latitudes, the flames expire, and palaces and quays and sea and sky fade to the myriad qualities of grey below the starlight. Soon in the town the lights spring up, and in the sky the light of a moon not yet risen on the earth: the one oar clucks and gurgles in the water, and coming near to the public gardens we hear the whirring of the cicalas and the tinkling of guitars and the rapture of nightingales. Some bell—in the month of May the bells of Venice are seldom silent—sounds from church or campanile.

But Italy was calling, and, after three weeks in Venice, sometimes I went across to the Ligurian coast to stay with Lord Stanmore in the Castello at Paraggi. A mile on the hither side of Portofino, and on the coast-road thither from Santa Margherita, a small headland juts out into the bay, and there, behind the gateway and lofty wall which cuts off the headland from the road, the sea-girt little castle, with cool, bare rooms and vaulted ceilings, stands in a garden shaded by pines, beyond the fringe of which the sun-bathed shore of rock plunges sheer into the sea. Though not so sharply hall-marked as Capri, this was authentic Italy, with dusty stone-walled roads where the lizards basked, and the terraced olives climbed the hill. Here, too, for me was born a new friendship, lighting another hearth of home in Italy, for one afternoon there came across the bay, in a red-sailed boat, the family from the castello at Portofino, Montagu Yeats-Brown, late consul at Genoa, and his wife, and their youngest son, Francis, home on leave from India; and the tentacles of friendship instantly shot out from his side and from mine. The art of scribbling was a passion with him, even as with me, and, no less, the love of the sea and the swimming and the basking, and presently we spent inseparable days among rocks and sea-caves, or climbed, perspiring, through the woods of chestnut and laburnum to the Portofino Kulm, and dropped down again to Santa Margherita, incessantly constructing stories and planning the great work of his about regimental life in India which would permit Rudyard Kipling to hand on the Oriental Torch and take a rest. He had an admirable, natural style, and that love of words, just for the sake of their inherent beauty, which marks off the true professional writer from the vague amateur, and later, when in the European war he was captured by the Turks in Mesopotamia, he wrote far the most vivid study in the psychology of captive life that has ever appeared.

Neither place nor persons can, singly, give the sense of home, though persons make home more than places: there must be some subtle mixing of the two before that atmosphere is created, but here was the mixing for me, and, another summer,

MOTHER

I settled down with him from May to August in that enchanted castle of Portofino. It stands, crowning the olive-planted cliff at the entrance to the harbour, looking down on one side over the huddled little town, and on the other out across the bay of Spezia. A wall of ancient fortification, enclosing the garden, tops precipitous rocks, by the base of which the path from the sea winds along an upward slope. Just hanging on to the seaward side above the pines, it joins the steep cobbled way from the village close to the entrance on the landward, and within are winding staircases in the solidity of the walls, and stone-floored chambers of coolness which the fierce heats of the summer cannot fever.

Many years before, Mr. Montagu Yeats-Brown had bought the place, then ruinous and roofless, while yet there was no railway along the coast from Genoa to Rome, and only a mule-track and the sea connected Portofino with the world. For years he went on with repair and reconstruction, and when it was habitable, he poured into it his wonderful collections of Italian furniture and porcelain. He had the curiosity and the omnivorous appetite of the true collector; a bronze implement, a dinner service from the *fabrique* of Sir William Hamilton at Naples, a stone axe-head, an inlaid *cassone,* an altar triptych, an obsolete centime-piece, were all irresistible to him. But chiefly he loved china, and glorious was his miscellany which swamped shelves and cupboards like a tide perpetually on the flow. He brought together, and eventually presented to the museum in Genoa, the finest collection of Savona jars ever made, and like all great collectors, he had occasional strokes of the most stupendous luck, as when, in a small shop in Genoa, he acquired for two *lire* a genuine piece of Medici ware, than which there is nothing rarer, except perhaps the pottery of St. Porchaire. His interest never flagged, and he must have been close on eighty when it struck him that no one had ever made a thorough study of china knife and fork handles, and he proceeded triumphantly to do so.

The dining-room and the paved hall opened into the garden, perched like an eyrie on the top of the cliff and surrounded with a low wall of old fortification. At one angle was some sort of sentinel outpost, from which, after dinner in the summer, you watched the alchemy of light in the withdrawal of the day and the dawning dominion of the stars. Often the sea was so calm that the reflection of a planet burned unwaveringly there three hundred feet below, and far across the bay the lights of Spezia were beaded along the horizon. The scent of stocks hovered in the air, and, still though it was, there was always a whisper of stir in the foliage of the stone-pine. And when this year the time came for my host and hostess to go back in June to England, Francis and I stopped on for a week, as originally intended, and after that for another week, and then, in true Italian fashion, abandoned intention altogether.

Every morning there was the long ritual of swimming and basking, and in the afternoon a rambling climb through the wooded hills, or if the wind was awake, a scudding across the bay in the red-sailed boat, and if (as usually happened) the wind then failed, long labours at the oar punctuated the perennial discussion of our future masterpieces. And then came dinner, begun in the afterglow and finished beneath the lights of stars and fireflies, and afterwards the hours of serious work, in some cool vaulted room, where, fatigued and exhilarated, we brought out the quires of scribbling paper, and he embarked on Indian adventures and I on the current history that engaged me. For two hours or three our agile pens streamed with creation and erasure, and then the ink began to flow less swiftly, and the cigarettes of rumination were multiplied. Then he or I would say, "Can't do any more to-night"; and after a swift disrobement we prepared the hammocks in the garden for slumber. These were slung to two stout branches of the stone-pine at the foot, and to the limb of a sumac that grew in the middle of the garden at the head. A rug below and a sheet above turned each hammock into a cool cocoon fit for summer nights, and the fireflies danced in the shadow of the pine, and the stars gleamed like minute golden flowers among the branches, and perhaps we talked for a little, but longer pauses succeeded to shorter questions, and we slid slowly into the dim regions of sleep. Sometimes we tried to keep awake in order to prolong the consciousness of exquisite environment, but part of the spell was the deepening of the drowsiness: to enjoy consciously was to lose half its magic.

Nature and our own imprudence sometimes played tricks with those tranquil nights; once in the small hours a thunderstorm stole up behind us over the sea, holding its breath in order not to wake us, and when it had got directly over our heads it exploded in a water-spout of rain and vulgar Wagnerian violence: it was a drenched helter-skelter that we made to the house. On another occasion we had only ourselves and rotten timber to blame, for just as I was falling asleep, I heard a muffled whisper from the foliage of the sumac at my head, and next moment the limb from which both our hammocks depended broke off short, burying us, like the Babes in the Wood, in an interment of leaves and branches. But when we had extricated ourselves from the debris, we found other less treacherous boughs, and thereafter the thunderstorms passed us by. And as long as I live I shall bear in my inward heart of happiness that nightly falling to sleep in the open, with the scent of stocks, and the drowsy pulse of the sea below, and the stars burning in the boughs of the stone-pine, and the black shadow of the castello lying across the white, moonstruck garden, and the sense of a drowsy friend in the hammock close by.

Another year, when Francis was in India, Venice was succeeded by a couple of months in Capri, which, years before, after my visit of almsgiving to Thessaly, had impressed its seal of home upon me. Now the stamping was to be made more materially secure, for I shared a solid anchorage with my friend, Mr. J. Ellingham Brooks, instead of floating on mere hotels and hospitality. At that time he had a nook built on the ancient wall of the town, with a tower in it, so that it came rightly by its name, the Villa Mura. A discreet door gave access to one of the cobbled ways, and within you found a little jungle of a garden that faced the house, high walled and cool, so that neither the stress of summer withered it nor would the winds of winter nip it. Fig-trees and nespoli-trees grew there, and bamboos and gigantic mallows: it was a forest in a yard. Apart from the tower, the house was a stone bungalow of one story, and from bedroom or dining-room or sitting-room you stepped out on to a minute paved terrace, and then plunged into the paths that led through a jungle fifty feet square. Here, so it seemed, was the sequestered corner of life which everyone at heart desires, and together we made plans for our joint ownership of it. Brooks lived in Capri all the year round, seldom setting foot on the mainland, and this would now be his permanent home, for hitherto he had moved from house to house in vagrant picnicking fashion, and I would spend the solid summer here, with encroachments into spring and autumn. But then, luckily before we made a fantastically cheap purchase, he had experience of a winter in the house, and the garden became a mere miasma and breeding-place of rheumatism, so that even his young fox-terriers limped and stiffened, and from the north aspect on the other side, so pleasantly refreshed by breezes in July, the *tramontana* of December beleaguered him with regiments of frozen bayonets, which stabbed to the bone the shivering victims. It was well enough for me who would only be there in the heat, but for him who had to face the winter there, it was no abiding-place. No ray of sun came to it, and he crouched over the fire with fingers too frozen to play his piano or transcribe his wonderful translation of Heredia's sonnets. So, during one more summer there we looked out for a less arthritic habitation, into which we could move before the agues of the autumn began. The subject was a pressing preoccupation, and we were conversing about it one evening as we came down into Capri, about the time of sunset, from the Tiberian palace on the top of the cliff that faces the mainland.

We were passing along a stretch of level path to the right of which rose a garden in three terraces, with a pine set in the middle and a pergola of vines running out at right angles to the house, which, two-storied and spacious, glowed in the liquid flame of the hour. A plumbago in full bloom climbed the white-washed façade, a balcony looked westwards high over the town below.

Though I had caught glimpses of the house before from the more frequented path up the hill, they had been but glimpses, and I had never seen it from this aspect, with its garden and pergola, and air of space and sun. But now it struck me that it was here and in no other house that we were to settle, and I asked Brooks for a précis concerning it. He knew it: it was a boarding-house kept by an English widow, and there was about as much chance of our getting it as of securing the moon, for in her capable hands it flourished with the same prosperity as did the garden under the ministrations of her brother, who boarded permanently here. It was no use, he told me, thinking about it at all, but my obstinate mind remained fixed in its quiet belief that Brooks and I were to live in the Villa Cercola. Sure enough, when I was in England again in the autumn, there came a letter from him, saying that this lady was giving up the house and would I telegraph if I wished to take a lease of it with him, for there were others desirous of it? In what suspense did I wait for the answer to my affirmative, and when it arrived, the lease of the Villa Cercola was ours with option to purchase.

The years went by since, in 1907, the shadow had

fallen over my sister's mind, and it had not passed away. A long and very critical period, in which none of us could see her at all, was over, but she had made no firm step towards complete recovery. Hugh and I, for some time, were the only people from outside who saw her at all, for a new and heart-breaking delusion had possession of her, that it was by plots and contrivances of my mother that she was prevented from going home. My mother, therefore, was advised not to see her at all while this was acute, for sometimes Maggie would not speak to her, and at other times was bitter and biting, and such interviews, so far from doing good, were very bad for both of them. My mother used to come back from them, yearningly and miserably unhappy, but still firmly clinging to the fact that it was just a bodily ailment, physical as a cold in the head, that caused Maggie's bitter ironies, and no shaft of them ever broke through that impregnable defence which love held. Her visits, however, ceased for a long period, but she constantly wrote to Maggie, with the news of Tremans, and just the assurance, serene and unshaken, that Maggie was under a mistake altogether about her, and that all the love and welcome in the world awaited her when she was better and allowed to come home. My mother always kept this before her, not insisting or pressing on it, but just quietly alluding to it, and though Maggie would often show me these notes, saying that they were all lies, yet she kept them all, every one, and sometimes when she answered them, with anger and flaunting sarcasm, she would say at the end, writing it very small, as if in whisper, " I wish I could wake up and find myself at home again," and those little, tiny words, hardly legible, meant everything to my mother, and all the rest was a troubled dream, as Maggie, somewhere within herself, knew : assuredly she would awake. . . .

I saw her at least every week when I was in London : usually I went down to Roehampton where she now was, and spent the afternoon with her, strolling about the big garden, and coming back to tea in her room. The cloud of depression and delusion was always over her, but, either because I had got to understand the physical nature of it better, or because she was tending towards recovery, there was no longer the sense of her being far away and out of eye-shot and hearing : sometimes she was so close. . . . Her mind, one began to see, was there all the time, liquid and clear : it was only on the surface of it that this grey ice of delusion was spread, and in herself she seemed often to know that the trouble was not real. Her memory was absolutely unimpaired, and by the hour we talked over detail after detail of the days when as children we made joint collections of plants and butterflies and birds' eggs. Always after a visit I received next day a letter recalling other memories past which our talk had slipped, the finding of the night-jar's nest, the capture of the first " Clouded Yellow " ; always, too, she would ask me if there wasn't any little thing that I wanted, and if I was unable to tell her of anything, she would think of something that our conversation had suggested to her. One day, for instance, mention had been made of the old poem, " Summer is i-cumen in," and by next week she had procured a little monograph about it with the tune to which it had been antiquely set : or, if she noticed I consumed chocolates with gusto at tea, there was a box of them for me to take away. She was sad always, sometimes vaguely blaming herself for all the trouble that had burst upon her : once only was she cross and disagreeable, and the next morning I received a note from her saying, " I can't think what made me say all those horrid things. I am afraid you won't come to see me again. . . ." Then it became possible for her to drive up to London with her nurse, and she often spent a couple of hours at my house in Oakley Street, or met Arthur or Hugh and went out with them. But always, when the time came for her to go back, there was the question, wistful but not insisted on, " Can't you take me home ? "

Over Tremans there fell another shadow, but clear and tranquil, without sadness. The beloved Beth, who had come as nursery-maid to my grandmother at the age of fifteen, years before my mother was born, and who had brought up the families of two generations, began to fail. She was now over ninety, and for nearer eighty than seventy years had performed her ministries of love, and none could remember a time when Beth was not piece and portion of home, and all that home had ever meant to any of us. She stepped about the house no longer to find linen that needed her darning needle, and from her bed she only moved on to her sofa and back again. She still liked my mother to read to her, but it was not now for the sake of the book, but for her presence and her voice. Beth would soon drop off into a doze, and at the cessation of the reading woke again, beaming all over her beautiful old face at the knowledge that my mother was with her. She had a nurse to look after her who for longer than the normal span of life had been nurse herself, but when any of her "young gentlemen," Master Arthur or Master Fred or Master Hugh (we none of us ever became "Mr." to Beth), was down at Tremans and came up to her room, as indeed they very regularly did, how quickly had Beth's nurse to leave her, so that she might have a talk to her young gentlemen alone. Another of Beth's young gentlemen paid her a visit now, and he was "Master Arthur" too, in spite of his grey beard and his more than seventy years, for this was Arthur Sidgwick, my mother's brother, whose birth Beth could remember. As he rose to go he kissed Beth, and then she was alert at once, and time rolled back the pages of more than seventy years, and he was a little baby again as she took his hand and kissed it. "Eh, and I've kissed your feet as well, Master Arthur," she said.

There Beth lay, serene on that high peak of life, and all the past was of one dim and sunny texture. For a little while she would be very wide-awake when her young gentlemen came to see her, and she talked of what "your papa" and "your mamma" had done and of a journey —she could not remember where—" when you were there, Master Fred, and Miss Maggie, but Master Hugh wasn't born."

" Was that the journey to Whitby ? " I asked.

" Yes, dear, that's it, Whitby ! And you were two years old and Miss Maggie was just turned four."

" I saw Maggie last week," said I. " She sent her love to you."

Beth's face beamed, and got troubled, and then beamed again. I think she knew only vaguely that something had gone wrong, and that Miss Maggie could not come in to see her. But she had sent her love.

Then Beth could not get to the sofa any more, and when next I was at Tremans, she had been in bed for a month. There was no more talk about Whitby and Wellington : she lay passive in the veiled sunlight which bathed her face, and whether that sunlight was of dim, happy memories as she looked back, or came from what lay in front of her, you could not tell. She had had some sort of stroke, which for a time disabled one side, but even as she lay sinking quietly away, power came back to her numbness. She suffered very little, and for six months more lay placid and content, though scarcely conscious, in the room plastered with pictures of her children of two generations. All her life she had given love, and all her life she had received it: there was never so blest and joyful a sojourning in the world which had never been a vale of woe to her: she would have scorned such a notion. She had followed one instinct, and that was devotion to her children; and knew one law, and that was love. And then, rather suddenly, one night came the final failure of her force, and the last face she saw and smiled at in the candle-light was my mother's, whom, seventy years ago, she had first taken in her arms. There was my mother by her now, not in Beth's arms, but Beth was in hers, and just as Beth had leaned over her, listening to her first breaths, so now my mother listened to those quiet, final respirations. There was no struggle at all, nor wrestling with an enemy. Beth missed a breath and clung a little closer to my mother's arm, and then she turned her face towards the beloved of her heart, and died. . . . And so I said that this shadow over Tremans was without sadness, for we all gloried in her serene passage. Out of the house which she had blest with her love she was triumphantly borne, and she lies now, the little that was mortal of her, in the churchyard at Horsted-Keynes, Elizabeth Cooper, aged ninety-two, and of a spirit quite ageless. We were all there but Maggie, and we talked of Beth as of one who had just gone round a corner on some new adventure.

Hugh, in those four years which intervened between Maggie's leaving Tremans and Beth's death in 1911, had entered on the final and busiest and by far the happiest period of his life. He had, within a year of his joining the Church of Rome, become a priest, and had gone to Cambridge, where he lived in Llandaff House with Monsignor Barnes, who had charge of the Roman Catholic undergraduates at the University. After a year there, he became curate at the Catholic Church, and lived for three years in the Rectory. But parochial work did not suit him, nor did Cambridge. For him a cold academic frost enveloped it, which for one of his temperament was far from surprising. In fact the only two things he liked about it were the river-bathing in the summer and, all the year round, his companionship with Arthur, with whom he struck up a new and extremely warm friendship. He was now rapidly becoming a notable preacher: he was also pouring out first historical and then modern novels with the furious haste that distinguished other members of his family. Novel writing was undoubtedly his passion, but with the work of a parish to do as well, for which he felt himself quite unsuited, he longed to get away from Cambridge, and order his life on a plan that had become his aim and ideal, and this was to live in a house of his own in the country and entirely to devote himself to preaching and writing. He wanted this with that particular kind of wanting which leads always to fulfilment, and his almost terrifying fecundity in authorship during these years was due (apart from the joy it gave him) to his desire to have enough money to live on, in case of some disaster happening to his power of earning a good income by his pen. With this end steadfast in the foreground of his thoughts, he saved every penny he could, rejoicing in the fact that he had not had a new suit of clothes for five years, and he made up for his one indulgence of incessant smoking, by buying the cheapest cigarettes that could be procured. And, indeed, to look at Hugh about that time was to wonder whether his clothes could be only five years old: greenish were they and of a reflecting surface, and his boots were such as you may pick up on the seashore, sticking out of the jetsam of the waves among seaweed and skates' eggs. But Hugh did not mind that, and, after all, he was the person principally concerned. Frayed cassock and bare buttons, if persevered in, brought him nearer to the realization of his dream: his books sold well, and increasingly better, and he began to shape the details of the delectable life. He made elaborate plans of the chapel he would build in the house of his dreams, and drew out his rule for the day, with the specified hours for meditation and worship and exercise and work. It was all in accordance with what he utterly believed to be, spiritually, the best mode of life that he could follow, and—here was the carnal joy of it—it was the sort of life which he preferred to any other.

Then one evening Arthur told him of a house he had seen for sale near Buntingford, in the course of a motor-drive from Cambridge, and took him over next day to see it. After a tragic moment of despair, in which Hugh bitterly lamented that he had ever set eyes on it, since it was exactly that and no other that he longed for, but would not possibly be able to afford, he found that he did afford it. It remained for him to get permission to drop parochial work altogether and devote himself to preaching and writing, and his hierarchs very wisely decided that it was the best thing he could do.

And thus, in the summer of 1908, when he settled into Hare Street House, Buntingford, the happiest and busiest period of his life began. He was at the height of his physical and mental powers, for, without very robust health, he had an amazing supply of nervous force, which propelled him along through seas of bodily and intellectual voyaging without any grating on shallows or grounding on shoals. In temperament he closely resembled in many ways R. L. Stevenson, for both alike were in absorbed and deadly earnest about their businesses, and at the same time treated life like some game of delightful adventure, playing with it even while they were so tremendously serious about it. If I had to put a short speech into Hugh's mouth which would just then best express him, it would be, "Oh, isn't it fun?" The actual writing of his books, the setting down of the words which had so much purpose behind them, was such fun, such glorious fun, and each book in turn, as it emerged from his pen, was, he loudly proclaimed, the best he had ever done: never was there such a book. If he was at Tremans, he would come hurrying and stammering into my mother's room with the new chapter crisply hot from the oven of his invention: "Mamma, I must read you this," he said. "It's g-g-gorgeous. May I have a cigarette here?" And (crowning convenience), though he intensely liked his critic's appreciation, he did not care at all if she found fault, for a poor benighted Protestant couldn't be expected to understand.

The moment a book was finished Hugh never gave another thought to it, for he was already busy at the loom of some other tale which would eclipse everything else. It was all such fun, and so deadly serious. The invariable idea and root-object in them all was to show the dealings of God with the men and women in the world He had created, through the Church which He had ordained; that was serious enough, but it was such a lark to do it, and to receive substantial sums of money as the result of hours which he could not possibly have enjoyed so much in any other pursuit. The same keen zest went to the making of his sermons: he set forth the glory of God, and he immensely enjoyed doing so.

But though the zest and fury of conviction inspired both book and sermon, the merits of the one cannot be compared to the merits of the other; in fact, what made the one marred the other. When Hugh preached, the flood of his thoughts carried you off your feet and swept you along with it; you could not stop and criticize, because you were for ever in the rapids, in the grip of his gesture and his eloquence, which were frankly irresistible, and there his genius lay.

But it was a different matter with the written and printed word, where the reader could go his own pace and not Hugh's. The inspiration was there (it was, indeed, exactly the same inspiration as illumined his sermons), but here it had hurried him along, while the reader, so to speak, was safely anchored to the bank, and could watch Hugh's headlong course, instead of being involved in it. In his own enthusiasm, and in his knowledge of what he wanted to convey, he was apt to make a sketch rather than a finished picture, leaving the reader to fill it in. And that is precisely what the novelist must not do: a novel is not impressionist (at least, it should not be) in the way that emotional speech is. The file and the polisher and the careful brush-work, which often, so far from helping the spoken word, only hinder it with the chill of academic finish, are absolutely necessary when the appeal is made, via print, to the leisurely eye. The setting, the characterization, above all, his treatment of human love, were often shadowy: all was a little misty till he came to the central scene, which was the salvation of a soul.

It is in the portrayal of human love, the heart's need of one individual for another individual, that there is the sense of something gravely wanting in his novels, and the reason for that is that Hugh never felt that need himself. In his sermons he went straight to the marrow and the pith, namely the human thirst for the love of God, and God's thirst for the love of man. Hugh knew that, he felt that, but he did not know the need of human beings for each other. His charm, his vitality, often strongly attracted others, but no one ever really took possession of his heart. He fully recognized this himself, and admitted that he had never entered into intimacy with anyone. He was always quite independent of other people, men and women alike (especially women), except as companions and playfellows. He was not in the least unsociable, but he never wanted anyone with the sense of thirst. If a friend was there, he greatly enjoyed his presence, and played croquet with him, but any friend would do, and if that friend went away, he did not miss him, but got another. And he thought of women precisely as he thought of men, but less so: sex, as a bewildering disquietude, never had any existence for him. Emotionally women meant nothing to him, nor, for that matter, did men. Of all women, the one he most enjoyed being with was my mother, and of all men, Arthur. It was not that the love of God so transcended in him all other emotion, that he had nothing fiery to give to his own kind, for he had always been like that. It was not either that he was an egoist, for egoists often love passionately for the sake of their own self-expression, and neither in that sense, nor in any other, was Hugh egoistic. It was pursuits of some sort that encompassed and enthralled him: he was both in boyhood and manhood always doing something with such fervour (and usually many things together), that he had no energy left for consciously being something, either lover or friend, still less enemy: for he never felt enmity towards others, and the enmity of others towards himself he did not so much despise as disregard to the verge of ignorance. The mere adventure of life, the fun of it, and the ultimate meaning of it, were his satisfying daily bread. His lack of strong human affection did not limit his capacity for compassion, and he had a limitless courtesy for the tiresome, while the one quality he loathed like the devil was any form of conscious cruelty. But he was always more tender to the helpless than to the efficient, and to animals than to people. He could not bear hurting a cat's feelings, because the cat could not respond by hurting his.

He brought his whole power of enjoyment to

the exciting business of acquiring and possessing this house and garden, for never before had there been a row of bricks or a square yard of soil that was his own. Now this most amiable dwelling, Georgian-fronted but Caroline within, and going back to the Tudor period, was his, and so, too, the spacious garden, and when he was not writing or engaged in his priestly offices, he was decorating or digging as if his whole energies were involved in panel or potato-patch. He saw in Hare Street House, for the years to come, his home and the resting-place of his old age, where, when the blood beat slower and the sinews were loosed, he figured himself quietly serene, waiting for the final call. Old age never came to him, and, for the present, anything less resembling rest or quiet, or the life of a contemplative or solitary, cannot be imagined. For he was never alone here : there was always somebody either living with him or staying with him ; and though certainly a " rule " existed which prescribed the set employment of the hours for mass and meditation, for correspondence and writing, it was, though serious, still part of a fascinating game. Silence, for instance, was to be observed from the hour of rising until noon, but the sporting side of this was that Hugh need not talk at breakfast, which he always disliked.

He, like most highly-strung people, felt little inclined for cheerful sociability early in the day, and the rule made it incumbent on him to follow his natural inclination. So he opened his letters at breakfast, but if there was anything amusing or interesting contained in them, he did not fail to communicate it.

His leisure was wholly devoted to the embellishment and cultivation of his house and garden, and when he was in residence at Hare Street, he hardly ever went outside his front gate. The first and prime provision was a chapel, and an old brew-house, which stood close behind the house, was converted to this purpose. He and Mr. Pippit, an artist friend who lived with him for a considerable time, constructed a roodscreen, and distempered the plaster between the beams of the walls: they carved on the beams the symbols of God's glory and His sacrifice, they painted the windows, they sewed the hangings, and Hugh, in some letter, describes with peculiar gusto the carving of the bracket on which stood the statue of the Blessed Virgin. Her foot was on the serpent's head, and beneath her writhed heresies with closed eyes and open mouths (because they will not see the truth, but proclaim falsehood), and devils with the heads of brutes.

And on festival days Our Lady wore a fine robe, and round her neck was a chain of jewels, which lengthened as Hugh acquired fresh moonstones and topazes. Reverence and religion were the true root of his labours, but what fun was the execution!

Then, still within doors, came domestic decoration. A border of appliqué work was fashioned to run round the walls of the oak-parlour where he wrote, representing the Quest and Attainment of the Grail, and round the walls of one of the bedrooms, which Hugh gleefully proclaimed should be reserved for Anglican clergymen, a perfectly ghastly tapestry representing the Dance of Death, horrible enough to steep the hapless occupant of this chamber in squealing nightmare. The great folios of the early Fathers, which twelve years ago my mother had taken from my father's library at Lambeth, and which, still augustly unopened, had followed the various moves of the family, were now carried off by Hugh from Tremans, as forming part of a suitable library for a priest, and were duly installed on shelves, and never taken from their places any more. Arras and panelling decorated the dining-room, and Hugh openly exulted that never a stitch had been put in all these hangings and tapestries by a woman's needle.

Out of doors in the garden there was no less scope for creation, for everything was neglected and overgrown and weed-ridden, and whoever was living with Hugh at the time must be ready to drop the needle or the chisel and cart gravel for the paths and dig the potato-bed. After the practical call of the vegetable garden, there were flowers to be cultivated, and a flagged terrace to be laid round two sides of the house. For other conveniences he had to employ professional artificers, who erected an engine that pumped water and produced electric light, and installed a central-heating apparatus. I was down at Hare Street the day after this last machine had been completed, and though it was tepid and muggy weather, Hugh had to turn on the full heat in every room, and our heads buzzed and our pulses grew quick and small. "Oh, isn't it lovely?" said Hugh, mopping his face.

At all these tasks he worked harder than anybody, and under the spell of his energy and enjoyment his guests toiled in his wake with blistered hands and scraped fingers, and the house and garden were filled with quaintnesses and delight. He had that wonderful sense of fitness which is called "taste" and gives charm to its manifestations: even the Dance of Death was charming, as fitly ministering to the uneasiness of Anglican clergymen. Never did he get used to Hare Street: up to the last day that he was there, it was to him a conscious exhilaration. But only rarely could he spend as much as a solid week there, for there was hardly a Sunday in the year when he was not preaching, or a span of week-days on which he was not lecturing, and thus his home was always new to him, a wonderful holiday-house, a house of dreams. There were often long absences from it: three times in the six years of his occupation he went on a lecturing tour to America, and three times he preached the Lenten sermons at San Silvestro in Rome. But in all available intervals he fled, like a homing-pigeon, to Hare Street, and there, amid other inconceivable activities, he poured out a stream of propagandist fiction.

And it all seemed to suit him so admirably : it is true that he was often very tired, but in early middle age it is right and proper to be tired before bedtime, if you have exercised a reasonable activity. After all, everybody has to go his own pace, and Hugh could no more have gone slow and avoided fatigue than he could have taken to an invalid life altogether. It was necessary for him (otherwise he would have been quite a different person) to fill every minute of the day with some mental or spiritual or physical exertion: he could not be different. Even his ailments had to be put in the stock-pot for future use, and when in 1913 he had to undergo an operation, he stored up his experiences, the waking on that morning, the pilgrimage to the operating-room, the linen cloth over the surgical instruments, with minute observation, and reproduced them all in a book he wrote immediately afterwards, dwelling with literary gusto on passages which at the time he had hated and feared.

But though this operation, in itself of a minor character, gave him complete relief from his malady, he was never quite the same again after it. Probably he was living already on the stretched circumference of his nervous vitality, and there was no reserve left on which to draw. He could not take a holiday, for he hated holidays, which, he said, always made him feel self-conscious, and as soon as he was discharged, he went driving on again, abating no whit of his activities: he never relaxed the bow, though the bowstring was deeply frayed. And when, less than two years afterwards, there came a sudden and unexpected call on his vital forces, there was no response: the frayed string snapped.

CHAPTER XI

THE family must certainly have been very trying to my mother during this year 1913, for, after a few months in India, which was a nightmare of increasing ill-health, I followed Hugh to the operating-table in May, and was severely but successfully dealt with. But these things passed: what did not pass was the cloud of confusion and depression which still hung round Maggie, and her bitterness and hostility. It was this, most of all, that began to tell on my mother: it was a background of darkness and of yearning, and though she still threw herself into the microcosm of village politics, and enjoyed with unbated relish the weeks she spent at Lambeth, not only did the minor maladjustments of life begin to fret her more than they had hitherto done, but its entertainments and pleasures to tire her. The limitations of age, for she was now over seventy, began to press more hardly, and though her spirit made light of them, for they were still but flimsy veils before the glow of it, they vexed the flesh. All her life talk and discussion had been in the very forefront of her joys, and now a growing deafness, never really serious, cut her off a little from the speed and precision which necessarily accompany talk.

She hated missing anything, and at the same time could not put up with the notion that people were raising their voices in order to bring her into full and accurate possession of what was going on. Though no one ever grew old with such skill and sweetness as she, it was a fact that she was doing so, and she found it a drag on the mental vitality which never to the end abated one atom of its eager elasticity. She wanted to see friends, to talk to them, to learn exactly and precisely all they had been doing and thinking, and how and why, to put them through the catechism of love just as minutely as ever, but the instruments of communication were beginning to grow a little dull, and she so much wanted to be bright and sensitive. She felt and deplored the inevitable limitations, even while her real mind recognized them as trumpery and in no way premature : she secretly dreaded disablements that never actually even threatened her. . . .

But of all this at the time, so bravely did she keep her colours flying, one saw hardly a glimpse, and it was only from subsequently reading the diary in which she recorded trivial events and happenings that I learned how constantly these limitations, which never became serious, irked her. The lid was firmly shut on them in her intercourse with any of us, except when she humorously alluded to herself as a tottering tortoise, and it was impossible at the time to imagine that she was finding that the wheels " drave heavily." She chose to consider these difficulties as trivial and despicable, and she concealed them with such success that we thought there was nothing being concealed, for on our flying but frequent visits to Tremans no jot of her vivid interest in our days and doings was abated. Whether one ought to have guessed that she was not as keen and confident as she appeared to be, I do not know, but most emphatically I am delighted that I did not. For she most clearly meant her private woes to be concealed from us: it was not her wish that they should have any footing in her life. Even if I had guessed, I should have been obliged to conceal my knowledge, for the reason that she put on the gallant face, and behaved as if they were not there. It was her wish that we should not guess: she did not choose to ask sympathy or comprehension in their regard.

She knew us all well enough to be aware how

we should have leaped to her had she given the faintest wave of a signal, but she wanted to be without woes in her dealings with us. These were things she meant to put away from her: she did not want sympathy with such rubbish. She preferred—and it was up to her—to be gay and keen, eager for talk, ready to laugh, to play bezique in the evening, as if nothing else mattered, and go reluctantly and brilliantly to bed. Then, safely private, she would confide to her diary how dreadfully she felt her loss of activity, her deafness, her "stupidity," and a mental disposition to criticize rather than enjoy. She talked to her diary, I think, somewhat as she might talk to her vicious green parrot, saying that she was a very dull old woman ("Aren't I, Joey?"). It was a sort of middle-distance talk; in the great shining background there was love, love of man and love of God, and all things that were holy and real to her, in the foreground the host of bright, pleasant details of which daily life consisted. Only, in the middle distance, was this muddy, sluggish stream winding wearily along. It bore the burden of increasing years, the unloosing of eager hands because the joints were stiff, and, more than all, the sense of the loss of enjoyment which, she was afraid, was curdling into a more critical tendency. But to us no signs of that appeared: she was just as deliciously greedy for news of our thoughts and scribblings, and she rejected in her life what she confided to her diary. It was a safety-valve, a blowing off of what might have condensed into discontent. " Get it down and have done with it," she once wrote, and when she had got it down, just for her own relief, she was ashamed of it. " But I won't go on like this," she hastened to add, " I WON'T, WON'T." . . .

Her growing love of the country also, of its peace and greenness and greyness, supplied a compensation to her fading delight in continual stir and movement. Neither in youth nor in middle life had she ever cared for it: she had inclined to Dr. Johnson's heresy that one green field was like another green field, and vastly preferred a walk down Fleet Street, where she would be in the jostling stream of men and women who lived and moved and had their beings and their businesses. But now, like Walt Whitman, she " had business with the grass " : flowers and trees and sedentary nature, so to speak, engaged her far more than ever before. Fascinating though people were, strangers and passers-by as well as friends, the stir of them and the prolonged intercourse with them fatigued her, and this fatigue she was learning to refresh and dissipate with the things that required no effort beyond contemplation. This changed and quickened interest is most marked in her diaries; again and again she now alludes to the beauty of the woods and lanes she walked in, whereas before they would have been an unheeded gymnasium for exercise and conversation : her companion would have absorbed her to the complete exclusion of her surroundings. It was not that she took any dimmer delight in people, for human intercourse always, up to the end, remained to her the supreme vehicle of mental activity, but she got more easily tired.

And always there was a want in her soul and a great yearning, for sundered by so few miles, but by such a sea of disordered delusion, was Maggie, still hostile. Her condition had improved sufficiently to allow of her being removed from Roehampton, and placed with fewer restrictions, under the care of a doctor at Wimbledon, but there could be no thought yet of her coming back to Tremans, where she longed to be, and where my mother longed for her to be. Once, for a short period, that hostility seemed waning, and there was an idea of turning a certain piece of the house into a flat, where she could be with her nurse. But the improvement faded again, and the doctors forbade the attempt.

But Maggie came back to Tremans once yet. The days passed for her now sadly, but very quietly, and, though still certified, she had much more liberty. And one day, when she was resting as usual in the afternoon, she got up, and, dressing herself to go out, left the house, and before her absence was noticed had slipped down the hill to the station of the district railway and taken the train for Victoria. From there she started again, remembering the change at East Grinstead, and, under the spell of this irresistible homing instinct, arrived at Horsted-Keynes, and set forth to traverse on foot the two miles and the steep hills which lay between her and Tremans. For years past she would not normally have been capable of such exertion, but now, in some exaltation of freedom and home-coming, the dusk and the distance did not hinder her, and she came down the avenue of pines, and out again by the farm-buildings and the orchard and the Egyptian lion-head, which she had dug up in the temple of Mut, and so to the door. On that summer evening it was open, and there was an old servant of my mother's passing between the kitchen and the hall. "I have come home, Mary," she said quietly, and went on into the house. . . .

Several hours before a telegram, agonizing to my mother, had arrived, saying that Maggie was missing and suggesting that she might have made an attempt to get home: meantime the search for her was going on. She was at home now, serene and composed, having accomplished what in normal health she was incapable of under this strong yearning and desire that admitted no obstacle. She spent the night quite quietly, and next morning, with my mother in attendance, went round the house, penetrating to every room, remembering all that was there, and pleased to find that her own room was unaltered. The doctor in whose care she was at Wimbledon had arrived late the night before, and she was now quite willing to go back with him, and seemed to know that she could not remain here. But she had had her will, and she was content, and went away again in some satisfied sort of triumph. She had seen it all once more, the shelter and the orchard, and the lion's head, and her own room, and after that clear gleam of sunshine, the clouds gathered again. But she had *got* to see Tremans again, and now she had seen it.

Then came the summer of 1914, with the ten

days of suspense as the great catastrophe grew no less incredible as it became inevitable, and, finally, the huge relief—no less—to know that England was at war. For already, across the tense and bitter years which followed, it is liable to be forgotten that the one thing, in those days, which seemed more terrible than a European war, was that England should stand aside and not be involved in it. France and Russia, our allies, were already in the maelstrom: at present we were on the bank.

On that momentous afternoon I was at a big party down in Essex: and there came for our host a telegram from the secretary of a large and well-informed London club. The Prime Minister's speech to the House of Commons was, at the moment that telegram was sent off, still in progress, and what reached us was the first part of it, in which he stated that our treaty obligations to France did not necessarily imply our embroilment. And there the message stopped.

The effect of that was that the whole party melted away: nobody could stand any more "party." But two hours later came the rest of the speech. An ultimatum had been sent to Germany which expired at midnight.

I had been fortunate enough to find a job of

war-work which would occupy me and perhaps be of some little use, and went to Tremans for a few days before settling down to it. It seemed impossible to realize that a European war, the greatest conceivable disaster that the mind had ever idly pictured, was then actually in progress. Of course, one knew it to be true, but with the same cold, unemotional knowledge as one knew it to be true that the brightness of a star-lit night was derived from suns fabulously remote : the mind had received information which it did not doubt, but the immensity of it baffled its power of assimilation. It was not that the fact produced any stunning effect, but that a thing so prodigious was insoluble at first by the acids of mental digestion.

Up in London it was patent, it was hammered into you till you believed it, but in these first days of August-tranquillity in the remote country, it was impossible continuously or convincedly to realize that the great cataclysm had arrived. There was certain evidence on the point in the daily papers, but they only arrived once a day, and for all the rest of the hours, the fragrance of dewy mornings, the chequered sunlight and shade of noon, the serenity of the clear twilight, all seemed to contradict that evidence, and made it impossible to establish in the mind that guns were already reaping a harvest other than that which now stood ripe on the golden Sussex weald. And even the news in the papers, which was all that the country-dweller had to go by, exhibited an optimism of which at first no one grasped the fatuity, for there seemed to be a hundred reasons for supposing that, bitter and bloody though the autumn might be, everything would be over by Christmas. Lord Kitchener, in whom the nation's confidence was rooted, was believed to have said that we were in for a three years' war, and, so ran the impression, he was quite right to lay his plans for an inconceivable contingency. But I imagine not one person in ten thought that he believed anything so utterly unimaginable. He wanted (and used bogey and turnip-ghost to get) an army of a million men not over thirty years of age. It was, of course, a ludicrous number, but naturally he desired to have plenty of margin. Then there were Liége, Namur, Antwerp, all guaranteed to be impregnable fortresses, which no enemy could leave untaken in his rear. There was the English fleet, which, blockading German ports, would speedily starve the Central Empires into submission, and, above all, there were the unnumbered hosts of Russia, which, if Germany attempted to drive back the Allied line on the Western front, would make an unchecked advance on Berlin. Russia, the relentless steam-roller (such was the universal phrase), was already on the move, and such armies as Germany could spare from the mere holding of the French front, could be no more than a crushed pebble on her road. . . . Then, later, when Liége and Namur the impregnable fell to the remote coughings of the huge German guns, and the tide of the German armies swept westwards as over level sands, the optimistic experts of the press grew more gleeful yet. Every day now, they whispered, the German lines of communication were lengthening : soon, as by a scissor-snip, they would be severed, and the great full flower-head of German armies would drop to the ground. Then came the magnificent rumour that Russian armies, the waste surplus of those who were steadily marching on Berlin, and for whom there was no room for deployment on the Eastern front, had been passing, in incredible numbers, through England to reinforce the West. Army corps of Russians were daily disembarking at Havre, at Dieppe, at Boulogne, and if you didn't believe it, you would soon see. . . . But behind these optimisms, behind the serenities and securities of the country-side, there was the sense of nightmare, not yet quite real. Only, as one began to awake, one realized that it was not of sleep that the nightmare was born, but of day and of reality.

In such sort of ignorance and miscomprehension did the country-dweller wallow during those early days of the war, when, sundered from all information except rumour and press-news hardly more reliable, Hugh and I were together at Tremans for the last time. He had already volunteered his services as chaplain, a prospect which he detested, but did not in the least shrink from, the less so, because he was inclined to look on the war as Armageddon, the mystic and final and futile stand of Satan against the heavenly hosts, which should be fought out, according to the Book of Revelation, on this planet. There were stories, too, of Angels seen at Mons. "It's extremely like Armageddon," he said, "and why shouldn't the Kaiser be Anti-christ? Besides, there's an eclipse of the sun to-morrow. It all fits in. 'The sun shall be turned to ashes.'" . . . Next day, sure enough, we had the eclipse, and noon grew sumptuously dark. And though Hugh strongly suspected that Armageddon was in progress, and the "great and terrible day of the

Lord " might be imminent, nothing could vanquish his invincible instinct of " playing," and he was marvellously absorbed in the fall of thirty degrees in the thermometer, in the device for observing the sun's disk in a pail of water, and in the phenomenon of the specks of light filtering through leaves, being no longer globular but crescented, reflecting, like little moons on the path, the shape of the uneclipsed portion of the sun. . . . And just when that cold twilight of noonday was at its dimmest, and the birds had tuned up, as at nightfall, and were silent again, there came the crunch of gravel underneath the bicycle of a telegraph-boy from the village, who delivered to Hugh the envelope he carried. Hugh tore it open, and the message announced the death of the Pope. . . . It was all Armageddoner than ever.

There was always a ceremony at Tremans when any of the family went away. The rest, who remained, collected at the front door from which the carriage was to start, and saw the departing person into it. He then drove off with his back to them, but the family waited till the vehicle reached the sharp angle on the drive a few yards away, which brought the carriage broadside on, and then he and they simultaneously made violent and encouraging gesticulations of farewell with their arms. Immediately afterwards the road passed behind the corner of the house and the voyager was carried out of sight. Just so did it happen when next morning Hugh went off. He whisked round the corner while we all threw up our arms and waved.

So, holding himself in readiness to go out any moment as chaplain, Hugh went homing to his blissful Hare Street, from which he issued for preachings and lecturings, returning again as soon as he possibly could. During the next few weeks he began, especially after any physical exertion, to suffer increasingly from spasms of pain, about which he consulted a doctor. These pains were declared to be those of " false angina," in no way serious, but severe while they lasted: there was nothing whatever wrong with his heart, either functionally or organically. Incessant smoking of cigarettes was discouraged, but Hugh did not pay any particular attention. . . . And there came to him the call, not that for which he held himself in readiness, but one for which he was just as ready. He neither expected it nor feared it, and when it came he seemed to welcome it, with such confidence did he look on the face of death. In October he was delivering a series of sermons and addresses at Salford, when these attacks of pain grew much more violent, though still in no way constituting any dangerous menace. Indeed, they seemed rather to be some strong warning, some bright danger-signal of nature, wholly friendly. It was with great difficulty that he got through the course, and he was leaving again for Hare Street, was, in fact, on the way to the station, when he felt himself physically unable to face the journey and went back to the Rectory at Salford for a few days of nursing and quiet. The pain was most intolerable when he lay down, and that night, seeking relief, he walked about his room, very lightly clad, and even went out into an open courtyard. Pneumonia developed.

A day or two later a telephone message from my mother, who was at Lambeth, reached me, saying that Hugh was seriously ill and that Arthur had gone to Salford. The doctors did not wish anyone else to come, for fear that Hugh should be made additionally anxious about himself by any further family arrival, and, indeed, there seemed to be no need. Only a few hours later came the final news. Without struggle or any mortal anguish Hugh had passed on, unquenched, taking that light of his round the corner, even as he had gone two months ago from the door at Tremans, with gay hands of salutation and farewell waving at us.

I went down next day to Hare Street, in order to find Hugh's will and ascertain whether he had left any special directions about the place and manner of his burial, which it might be necessary to telegraph to Arthur at Salford. Everything had been made ready in his house for his return, which had been expected three days before, and the place seemed indescribably full of him; he had surely arrived, and was looking round. Was there not a subdued tinkle from the piano in the library? was not that a step on the stairs? Or perhaps he was out in the garden, seeing what progress had been made with the rose-bed. As, in the early-fading light of that grey October afternoon, I searched for his will through locked drawers and likely places, I must have looked up a dozen times to see whether he had not naturally and noiselessly entered. And then, still not finding it, I turned to a pile of papers on his writing-table in the parlour, round the walls of which ran the Quest and the Attainment of the Grail, and there it was, on the top of them, as if before he went away he had arranged that it should be easily accessible. It was strange that he should have placed it there, but, as far as I know, he had no presage of his death when he left Hare Street.

He had left elaborate and curious wishes respecting his grave. He wanted, if it was possible, to be buried in a brick vault in his garden at Hare Street, over which, at some future time, there would be built a chapel. He directed that his coffin should be of light construction, easily broken from within, and there was to be placed close to it a duplicate key of the vault. If it was impossible to follow these instructions, he directed that a vein in his body should be opened before he was buried, so that it might be made certain that he was dead. As he lay dying, he repeated this wish to my brother.

I do not think that this dread of Hugh's with regard to being buried while in a state of suspended animation, now for the first time made known to us, can have been anything like a real " phobia," an unreasonable, fixed obsession. Even while he wrote these directions, I feel sure he must have been " playing." . . . With what gusto (it seemed as clear as if we had discussed it together over the fire) must he have elaborated his plan of the light coffin and the duplicate key. " There'll have been the mass in the chapel," I could almost hear him saying with his eager stammer, " and then you'll b-b-bury me and lock the door of the vault. And that evening you'll be sitting here in the parlour, and you'll hear a t-t-tapping on the window, and when you go to see what it is, there'll be Me in my robes and b-b-biretta, with the end of my nose quite white from being pressed against the glass. And then you'll think it's my g-g-ghost, but it won't be, and so you'll let me in and we'll have supper. What awful fun. . . . 'Tisn't playing with death, because I shan't have been dead at all, and I'll write a book about it."

So I felt then (and feel still) that, in spite of some touch of "phobia" about being buried alive, he vastly enjoyed writing these directions: it would be a thrilling adventure. He had no doubt vaguely intended to build this vault, but he had not done so, and it was now clearly impossible to contrive everything as he had planned: indeed, his request to Arthur that his death should be made quite certain showed that he recognized this. All that could be done was to obtain permission from the Home Office that he should be buried in the garden with a view to the subsequent erection of a chapel, such as now stands there, over his grave. This permission was given, and, after his death had been made sure, his body was brought from Salford to be buried close to the rose-plot over which he had been so busy that autumn, and there he was laid in his own garden. In the chapel which had been Hugh's first care when he came to Hare Street, the mass for the dead was celebrated by Cardinal Bourne, and sung by members of the Westminster Cathedral choir, and in a tree by the grave-side a robin was joyful.

The whole of this little domain which Hugh loved more than any spot on earth, Hare Street House, with the garden and another house he had already built on the property, was bequeathed by him, with a suitable endowment for upkeep, to the head of the Roman Catholic Church in England at the time of his death and in perpetuity to his successors. Everything in the house, except for a few named objects and a little choice of mementoes for friends and relations, was included in the bequest, and so there will ever be this strange thing, that in the house of the head of the Roman Catholic Church in England will be found several pictures of Archbishop Benson of Canterbury and many volumes of the early Christian Fathers from his library.

There was a curious sequel, for Hugh's will was found to be invalid, not having been properly witnessed. He was therefore adjudged to be intestate, and the whole of his estate, including, of course, Hare Street, passed to his next of kin, his mother, his brothers, and his sister. So, in order to carry out his wishes, we were obliged to have a friendly law-suit with Cardinal Bourne, by which the whole property passed into our possession, and then we gave it back to him. I mention this because there was an impression that we fought the will in order to deprive Cardinal Bourne of the bequest, but we must disclaim all such splendours of ultra-Protestantism, for the facts were precisely the opposite. The suit was necessary in order to enable us to give possession of Hare Street to those for whom Hugh had intended it, and it is now, and will always remain, the property of the head of the Roman Catholic Church in England.

In times of great sorrow and intimate bereavement my mother, all her life long, had ever soared above the cloud and found the brightness, and it was so with her at Hugh's death. For many months she had been anxious about him, feeling that nobody, especially if he was not physically robust, could " go on " as Hugh was doing without a breakdown, and indeed, in the sunshine of her faith, she feared death for herself and for those she loved less than she feared the hazards of life. Illnesses, anxieties, perplexities were entangled with the mere act of living: you were in a net of knots and enmeshment from which there was but one release, since, as long as you lived, you had to do your best with constraining circumstances.

But she was utterly at peace with regard to death; death was not puzzling, but simple and big, and though she loved life, and loved that those she loved should afford her the sweetness of their presence, so many of those she had known longest, and into whom she was most closely knit in soul and spirit, had by now passed over the little ferry that could not be very far ahead on her own marchings. It was thirty-six years ago that her eldest son Martin had died, and even then, in the plenitude of her health and activity, she had hailed God's will, not with submission, but with welcome, and now that welcome was serener yet, and less difficult, by reason of the counterpoise of earthly ties and considerations of attainment. For Martin had died in the promise of his brilliant boyhood, with all his gifts and possibilities yet in the bud, but now there was no such ground for struggle in her acceptance. Hugh was young still, but for years now he had overworked and over-strained himself, and had he recovered, there must have been a long and tedious convalescence, such as it was impossible to imagine as tolerable for him, and even then no return to that whirl of activity and pressure which really seemed the only atmosphere in which he could breathe. He was now safe in the heart of the infinite Love, and she feared for him no longer. With her whole soul she had longed and prayed for his recovery, but somehow this was better yet. Just because her heart was so big and her faith so burning, and because, too, it could not be very long in the measure of years till she would see him again, she looked on his death as she might look, a little dazzled, on an added brightness in the sunset towards which she moved.

It was the living for whom she feared, and, of these, most of all for Maggie. There had been a hope there; for only a day or two before Hugh's death, she had undergone an operation, serious but not dangerous, which, if successful, might perhaps have revealed and relieved the source of the trouble. But the hope was not realized, and for some days yet, as she recuperated, it was not possible to tell her about Hugh. But when it was permitted, I went down to Wimbledon; she had been moved to a sofa from her bed, and, when she knew, we talked for an hour about him and his love for her, and his funny ways when he was little, and his disobedience to Beth, and the lessons which Maggie taught him. There was his paste-board armour covered with silver paper, his habit of crying "Pax" when, having insulted an elder, vengeance was imminent, his conversion to another Church, his house at Hare Street, the tiny pond at Tremans which he tried to stock with perch, his unspeakable boots. But most of all she recalled memories from his boyhood, with little gleams of smiles breaking through her sorrow. She was completely herself that afternoon, without blame or displeasure or delusion. . . . And then the rent clouds blew over her again, and the storm beat. But there had been just that little remission.

CHAPTER XII

THE optimists of the press, who had so gleefully prognosticated that there would be peace by Christmas, owing to the Russian steam-roller in the East, the cutting of the enemy's lines of communication in the West, and the sure starvation of the Central Empires from the strangle-grip of the English fleet on sea-traffic, were chirping rather less vociferously (like the birds on the noon-day eclipse in August), and wondering if Lord Kitchener really meant what he said. The German lines of communication were still intact, no news of starvation came through, and the only steam-roller that appeared to be taking any part in the proceedings was that of the German armies, which had crushed their way over the north-east provinces of France. There was no abatement of patriotism, no loss of courage or lowering of the heart held high, but during the next spring it began to be realized that we were not in for a short and terrific combat, but for a struggle long and bitter beyond all previous conception: there grew the sense that the war was not to be won by one swift, magnificent stroke, such as the early optimists had encouraged us to hope, but by sheer endurance.

The only contribution of help that civilians—women and men over the fighting age—could make was a strict attention to such work, however infinitesimal, that had been allotted them. Most of them were beginning to find the unaccustomed routine quite intolerably dull, and they discovered that (wholly apart from the great issues, from the horrors and sorrows and splendours) the war was, above all things, the most frightful bore. As the year went on, its boring quality steadily increased: the lights of the city were darkened in view of air-raids; the train services, whenever you could get any, were so curtailed that the guard's van was often the only place where you could find standing-room; food-supplies were rationed, meat, sugar, butter, occasionally bread, were reduced to derisory measures; matches were often unattainable; whisky, as by some inverted miracle, we turned into water; prices rose, and so did the income-tax; books would not sell; ladies with trays of flags blackmailed you in the street; all the comforts and amenities of life, in fact, which had hitherto been phenomena, as regular and as natural as the rising of the sun and the setting of the moon, dropped off the stem of existence like withered autumn leaves. Excitement, pleasurable in itself independently of its cause, could not permanently remain at fever pitch : you could not go on for ever reading edition after edition of the evening papers as they came out, and excitement was boiled down into a glue of anxiety and depression, which rendered the minor discomforts of life doubly irksome. By degrees the wiser part of the civilian population, instead of thinking about the war all the time, strove to do its war work, whatever it was, as efficiently as possible, and, as far as possible, not to think about the war. So London generally finding itself quite ignorant of what was really going on, did its tasks, and settled down in a truly English spirit, to make the best of discomforts, among which air-raids began to be numbered, and bethought itself of the wisdom of Queen Elizabeth, who in the days preceding the Spanish Armada, pronounced that "there was need of mirth in England now." The disasters of 1915 and the two and a half years which followed were not lessened by pulling long faces, nor by listening to the numerous ravens who croaked unfounded tales of woe, and those with any grain of sense set themselves to enjoy all that they possibly could.

If the news, such as was vouchsafed, was good, there was an added cause for cheerfulness; if the news was bad, they danced and played bridge when their work was done, with a determined detachment wholly admirable. The working hours of the day were for me taken up in certain businesses, some dull, some interesting, such as the study of the affairs first of Turkey and then of Poland, with a view to the enlightenment of the public regarding these arenas, and when the day's work was done, and my brain bewildered with marshalling facts in such a way that difficult and complicated situations might appear simple to the reader, I made my daily escape in the evening into scenes and years as remote as possible from the environment of war. I shut and locked the door, and went back into boyhood with David Blaize. Over him I must be pardoned for lingering a moment, for, however trifling the result, I have never in all my commerce with scribbling, found in the process so potent a Lethe for the current pains and pleasures of conscious existence.

I had long wanted to write some kind of chronicle concerning a boy's adolescence, when for a time, shy and impressionable and vastly sentimental, he belongs to neither of the two sexes, and does not melt into his own sex for a year or two yet. Some boys, rather rare exceptions, are thoroughly male throughout this period, but most are of some strange third sex, lively but quite indeterminate. Just at that age everything is fiery; the proper human boy, who is on the way to become a man with stuff in him, whether for the building of empire or the amelioration of slums or the more ascetic devotion to art, touches life with a burning finger. His affections and friendships, like his cricket or butterfly-collecting, are passions to him. With girls the same general principle holds good, but with this difference, that a girl is far more a little woman than a boy of corresponding age is a little man. Her sex has more definitely declared itself than his, and though the normal girl makes passionate friendships with those of her own sex, she is always imagining herself a woman with marriage and wife-hood and child-bearing dimly in front of her. Two girls, in fact, will confide to each other, in virgin intimacy and innocence, the glories of a boy, but two boys of fifteen or sixteen, in similar circumstances, will not so often rave over the wonder of a girl. The riddle of sex bothers them less, the expression of it more, but they have a compensation in the greater outlets for energy that they enjoy. Boys (the energy of the sexes being taken as equal) can blow off their steam over games, which to girls are more a recreation than an aim. There is, though boys are just as sentimental as girls, a larger sluice, the joy of running and hitting.

In both boys and girls then about the time of adolescence, there occur these signs and signals of love: an adoration, that is to say, and a devotion wholly transcending the normal limits of friendships. In an adult they would rightly be termed abnormal, but at an earlier age they are so common that we must regard them as a stage in ordinary natural development. But the whole subject from the male point of view was somehow tainted with beastliness, or guttered away into mere tallowy slosh; if rash people wrote a story about school-boys and touched on their affections, they seemed at the most to set their climax at the school-concert, where the small boy (treble) sang "Oh, for the wings of a dove," and felt that he was singing at the captain of the school cricket eleven, who, eighteen years old, blue-eyed and golden-haired, had made a century that day, and was sitting next the head-master's daughter, whom he married afterwards. Sometimes the younger boy contracted consumption, and, as in *Tim*, was carefully kissed by the elder shortly before he died. Otherwise, school stories, if more discreet, were even more blatantly unreal: there were cheats and bullies (Group I) and cricketers and noble young people (Group II), and the cheats were detected and degraded to lower forms, and the bullies were birched, and all the cricketers made immense scores, and all the noble young people got scholarships at Balliol.

But why not try, so I had long thought to myself (and probably fail), to write a school story not about cheats and bullies and sopranos, to deal with affairs that conceivably might have happened : to imagine a boy clean-minded and instinctively revolting from sentiment, who is yet absorbed in such passionate friendship as is characteristic of the fiery age ? There was no need to get rid of the captain of the eleven, for he invariably occurs in real life, nor of normal boys madly keen on cricket and friendship, who, though loathing the expression of sentimentality, were, nevertheless, profoundly sentimental. All this had churned in my head for years past, and now, just now, what completer escape from the tragedy and boredom could a scribbler find ? It was to be boyhood again before war was invented or sex manifested, when four copper coins would infallibly produce a pound of sugar, when perfect bliss could be enjoyed with half-a-dozen racket balls and a friend, and when anyone over the age of twenty seemed already ripe for the winding-sheet.

And then, with half a page written, and the half page torn up, and a page written and the page torn up, the door at which I was thus rapping swung open, and let me in to a domain where I had no need to invent but only remember and rediscover. For there, in the forest of years in which my boyhood had wandered and lost itself, I seemed to find it again, quite alive and happy and ready to talk, and the whole business of recording appeared to be taking down the dictation of some external agent. Of course there was no external agency, but some internal and subconscious clamouring of memories which had so long been forgotten by my conscious self that they wore the garb of discovery. Now the door of that storehouse was open and it was lit within and full of lively folk, and chapter after chapter came bubbling on to the paper without effort or selection or arrangement on my part. The lively folk had settled it all among themselves: I had only to put down what they told me. So, on most evenings for six months or more, I locked out the war and tiptoed back to where David and his friends were waiting for me. . . . When it was published, I found, with a thrill of amazed pleasure, that at last I had written something which my mother hailed and rejoiced in.

During the spring of 1915 she began to be aware in herself that the hope of Maggie's recovery was growing dim. Mentally she was better: it often seemed that the mists were very thin: she was separated by clouds that stirred and shifted. There was less blame, there was a softened hostility: Hugh's death seemed to have shaken her enmities. But, though up to the time of her operation last October her physical health had been very good, that rock, on which we relied for the rebuilding of her mind, now began to totter: disquieting symptoms appeared, and her heart showed signs of weakness. Hitherto she had often come up with her nurse from Wimbledon to my house, and the change of scene, the fact of free re-entry into normal life had refreshed her. But now these excursions became rare, and it was oftener that I went down to Wimbledon instead, for the drive and the change of scene tired rather than invigorated her. Still, now and then, on good days, she came, and so thin sometimes were the mists round her that for an hour or two she seemed wholly normal, rather sad, but with no burden of heavy melancholy or disordered thinking. But physically she was weaker, not alarmingly, but increasingly.

Then in August there came a crisis which, as one saw afterwards, gave the key to the manner in which would come the end to her imprisoned darkness. She had an attack of syncope, but with that tenacity to life which nearly twenty years ago in Egypt had almost miraculously enabled her to turn and come back out of the very gate of death, so now, with mind suddenly serene and clear, she fought her way through it, and asked to see her mother, to whom, in this bitter dream of estrangement, she had so long imagined herself to be hostile. In a few hours she was there, and Maggie was just an ailing child again, wanting her and finding her. The cloud had lifted, and disclosed Maggie exactly as she had been before ever the trouble came. . . . In childish days, when she took her worries to the heart that never failed her, she, when the comforting talk was finished, used often to kiss her and say, "Oh, Mamma!" and Mamma said, "Oh, Maggie!" and then they laughed. And now when her mother, sleeping in the house, left her to go to bed, Maggie sent her nurse with a message to her, asking her to bring back her mother's reply. The message conveyed by the nurse was just, " Oh, Mamma ! " and when Nurse Holt came back from her errand Maggie asked, " And what did she say ? " Of course she had said, " Oh, Maggie ! "

And then, as Maggie grew physically stronger after that attack, the clouds grew thick again. The tragic, disordered hostility returned, and a few weeks later she thought that she knew how mistaken she had been in believing that there was love between them. But those few hours had been tonic to her mother, for now she knew, not by faith only but by experience, that Maggie was *there* all the time. She had never really doubted it, but Maggie had been absent from her so long : now, for a moment, Maggie, her very self, had come to her. That gave her confidence during the few months that were yet to pass before the last mists dissolved, leaving the serenity of love undimmed.

It was in May of 1916 that the final light and deliverance came. All the winter Maggie had been losing ground : her heart could no longer stand the ascent of stairs, and her bed was moved into a big sitting-room on the ground-floor. There were but a few steps down into the garden, and in that spring of loveliest blossom she often sat out there. She had taken up her sketching again, and made sad, pale little pictures, and she had collected and revised for publication some tales about animals which she had written before her illness. Intellectually her faculties were as alert as ever, her memory and her critical powers were unimpaired, but delusions were thick and dense. . . . One afternoon, for instance, she had been telling me in hushed tones that there were several people—" not quite people "—talking together in the corner of her room, and boding no good to her, but she was willing, though with misgiving, to say that she was not really quite sure about this invasion, and we went on talking as usual of Beth and Hugh and the distant days at Lincoln and Truro. That afternoon I did not stop very long with her, for she was tired, but I promised to come back to-morrow.

And when next day I came, Maggie was there, she herself. . . . Her nurse had gone into her room that morning, and she was still sleeping, but presently she awoke, and smiling at her, she said, " Eureka ! " She asked for the doctor and his wife, and when they came, she told them what she had found, and it was that all was healed, and that there was nothing in the world except love. She thanked them for their care of her: she wanted to know if her mother might come to see her.

That was how I found her in the afternoon:

"Oh, this is nice," she said. "Come and sit close by me. Look, I am wearing the little Egyptian lapis-lazuli bird you gave me. They have promised never to take it off my neck: never."

I do not think I have ever been happier than I was then. I knew that Maggie could not be many days with us: she might, perhaps, be only a few hours, but before she went she had come right out from the darkness and the prison, and was free. She smiled at the memory of my visit yesterday.

"I can't think why I supposed there were people in the room," she said. "There was no one but you and I. Can you stop here a long time to-day? Mamma is coming: she will soon be here now."

We talked on, and presently my mother arrived, and on her face was a joy past telling. Last year, for a little, the cloud had parted, but it had formed again: now it had dispersed altogether, and Maggie had gone back to years long past, when there was no such friend as she who sat beside her now. All next morning my mother was with her, and they never spoke of the last nine years of deluded estrangement, but only of their love, and of Love itself from which that flame was kindled.

Then once more came my turn : there had been a bowl of lilies of the valley by her bed, but just before I came in, she remembered that, by reason of a childish biliousness, I still disliked the smell of them, and in the doorway I met her nurse who had been asked to carry them away. And after a little Maggie wanted both of us together, and then my mother alone. She, when she left, was under promise to come again quite early next morning, and Maggie said she would settle down for the night very soon, so as to be ready for her.

Once in the night she woke, and her nurse heard her say over the first verse of the hymn, "As pants the hart for cooling streams." Then she went to sleep again, quiet and happy, and without movement or struggle her breathing ceased, and her eyes opened on the everlasting day.

I do not suppose that to the end of my mother's life a single day passed on which there was not in her mind the memory of those last hours with Maggie and the sweet miracle of her restoration. She would, in any case, have looked on her death as a release, but this complete and serene return before the end, made just the whole difference, for it utterly expunged the bitter and bewildering years. They were annihilated: it was to her as if they had never been, or, at the most, they were of texture unreal as a dream, that faded in the dawn and dayspring of death. All through she had told herself that Maggie was there, and now in the final triumph Maggie had come herself to ratify the truth of her steadfastness. . . .

In the autumn I began to be busy, in a branch of the Foreign Office, with collecting materials about the enemy's position in Turkey, where with an incredible thoroughness and industry the Germans were rapidly assuming complete control over military, naval, political, industrial, educational, and financial affairs. Turkey was already a helpless vassal, having been deluded into this serfdom by Imperial promises of the construction of an Ottoman Empire which was to stretch on the East to the boundaries of China, to include vast Volga provinces, and embrace the whole of Egypt. Beautiful German maps, which I studied with ravished attention, were already in widespread circulation throughout Turkey, showing into what world-wide dominion she would leap at the victorious conclusion of the war. German officers were drilling Turkish troops, German engineers were completing the Taurus tunnel on the Baghdad railway, and a trans-European express was running from Berlin, advertised and labelled as the " Baghdad Express," though I do not think that before the end of the war (and certainly not afterwards) it went any farther than Constantinople. Germany instituted Boy Scouts in Turkey, who would soon become German soldiers fighting Germany's battles, she brought under cultivation thousands of acres to supply food for the Fatherland, she made docks and quays and reservoirs : she even produced a Turkish national poet who wrote magnificent patriotic odes to Attila: "My Attila, my Huns" is the fine opening of one of these, which thus ingeniously couples together ancient invasions of Europe from the East with the Western invasion of Europe from Prussia. In all such propaganda, Germany chiefly employed Jewish agents, just as she did in raising the Russian revolution, and this poet Tekin Alp was a Semite from Salonica.

The Turks, in that strange mixture of barbaric ignorance and of high-breeding which characterizes them, swallowed, incredible though it sounds, all these preposterous baits. Their ignorance permitted them to believe that they were capable of becoming a great Empire : their innate gentlemanliness refused to credit that their high-born ally, the Emperor William, would not keep the promises he had made to those ruffians Talaat and Enver Pasha. As a matter of fact, of course, Germany was getting, and by the end of 1916 had got, complete control of all Turkey's internal affairs. Turkey was a German province magnificently organized and completely dependent on the Fatherland. There were, however, significant symptoms of a want of confidence in these golden dreams woven by Germany for her dear ally, for Talaat and Enver, secretly hedging, had withdrawn from the Deutsche Bank in Constantinople the whole of their own private fortunes and of the funds of the Young Turkish Party, the Committee of Union and Progress, and had converted them, at 50 per cent. loss on the exchange, into Swiss francs, lodging the balance at Zurich.

By the summer I had, as far as I could judge, sucked dry all possible sources of information on my subject, and it was necessary to leave other work alone, and to assimilate and classify these facts, in the hope of producing an intelligible volume exposing Germany's little plans. Some "villegiatura" in the country seemed desirable, and even as I said " villegiatura " there leaped into my mind the image of my white house in

MOTHER

Capri, with the stone-pine whispering in front of the windows. Oh, for the sun and the South! Oh, to take bundles and sheaves of notes, and Tekin Alp's poem, and a map of the future Turkish Empire, and a little private memorandum from Zurich about certain funds, out to the white villa on the enchanted island, and there clarify and scribble! I wanted very much indeed to do that: I sat down and wanted it.

Now, if you set yourself to want anything with the right brand, the effective quality of wanting, you usually get it. You must not dissipate your energy in frenzied fussing or widowish importunity: you must want in a certain quiet and deadly fashion, ready of course to take hold of your chance when it approaches, but with no hasty grabbing movement; it is as when you seek to catch a horse that is loose in a meadow. I give no explanation of this; I understand it no more than I understand cyclones and lunar revolutions and other examples of natural forces, but I am aware that they are founded on fact. I feel sure that if you want in the correct manner, you will get. . . . It happened just like that now: a friend in the Foreign Office wished for something—here discretion takes command—to be conveyed to Rome, and simultaneously a friend in another department desired a little information which could best be ascertained at Rome: I was perfectly ready to convey the one and ascertain the other.

And so one evening, after some interesting conversation in Rome, and the delivery of an object at the Embassy, and after the dispatch of a dozen pages of closely-written facts and surmises to London, I saw again the enchanted island outline itself against the molten flames of sunset on sea and sky. Italy now had abandoned her neutrality, and, though seething with very remarkable German intrigues, was committed to the cause of the Allies. But, as ever, the few miles of sea which separated Capri from the mainland, were Nepenthe and Lethe, and disembarking from the waters of oblivion, I could scarce believe, save for my sheaves and bundles of Turkish jottings, that there was any war at all. The papers, it is true, brought news of it, when there was not some strike of post or printers, but the sound of its roaring was no more than the echo of the sea in a shell, and the machinations of Talaat and the manœuvres of Enver seemed, as I began to tackle them again, like some fantastic history of goblins and highwaymen. But for the chronicler such detachment was all to the good, the business had gained perspective, and could be contemplated and explained with equity. The chief difficulty was to make it plain and easy. Anything easy to understand can so readily be made complicated by elusive narration, for the air of mystery and bewilderment is sooner woven than any other. But it is far more baffling to take a tangle and straighten it out into a clear skein without knots or impediments to smooth running, and the reward of success is to read it, as I did, to a victimized friend, and hear him say, " But it's all pretty obvious, isn't it ? " So here again were the mornings and the noons and the nights of enchantment, the windless southern summer, the ripe figs and the lizards basking on the walls, and though I have no disordered desire for figs, and no passion for lizards, nor any imperative internal need of swimming in warm seas and dining under a pergola, the sights and the sounds made up a spell, and it was the old gay spell of Italy. Meat on the island was hard to get, and harder yet to eat, the bread seemed to consist of shingle and minced wood, so instead of your toast or your chop you ate some peaches. Ruefully I regarded the progress of my writing, and the pages of notes on my table ebbing away as I snowed the torn remains of each embodied leaf into the waste-paper basket, for the end of my work was the end of my days here, and I must get back to the fogs and the grime. But there were red-letter days of respite when I could not make much headway, and even better was it to be taken aback, and forced to re-write instead of going forward : I have never been so conscientious a constructor.

The conscientious constructor had a very agitating moment on the platform of the station at Rome on his return journey. I have an inaptitude for packing clothes in travelling bags and trunks, which amounts to a positive deficiency, and when I came to the bestowal of my effects in the cases in which they had been packed for me, they were choked and gorged and unlockable, while shoes and shirts and manuscript still lay profusely waiting. The only remedy was to get another receptacle, especially since I knew that I was to convey a bag of dispatches from the Embassy at Rome to the Foreign Office. I remembered that I had left a suitcase here, which I had taken to India a few years before, and there, sure enough, I found it in the box-room, and I bundled my overflow into it, and found that there was still plenty of room for the bag of dispatches. . . . Two evenings after, there was I on the platform at Rome with the dispatches and my completed manuscript on Turkish affairs inconspicuously housed in the suitcase which had been to India. As I stood waiting for the conductor of the sleeping-car to verify the number of my cabin, I suddenly observed that this suitcase, with its precious and private contents, was incomprehensibly attracting a good deal of attention : there was quite a crowd forming round, with pointed fingers. Then with a positive pang of horror I grasped the reason, for I had sailed to India from Trieste in an Austrian-Lloyd steamer, and there, intact and flaming on the end of my suitcase, was a hotel label and a luggage label of that accursed town.

It was a wonderfully disagreeable moment: there was I, wanting only to shun publicity and objecting very strongly to have any attention called to that particular package by reason of its contents. I purported to be carrying dispatches for the British Government, as my passport would show, and all the time my luggage mutely and distinctly testified that I had come from a port in the enemy's country. Forged passport, spy, Tedesco were words that vividly occurred to me, as no doubt they were occurring to that interested group of persons round my suitcase. I snatched it up from the gaze of curious eyes, and retreating into the sanctuary of the sleeping-car, with clawing nail and jabbing pen-knife I scratched to shreds those labels (so liable to be misunderstood), and threw the fragments out of the window. But I had no idea until then how durable was the quality of the gum on labels, or how pleasant, under certain circumstances, it was to find your train in motion. . . .

That July, while Arthur was at Tremans, once more the demon of acute depression attacked him, and drove him into a rest cure where he wretchedly remained for many months. So when the Christmas gathering at Tremans came round, we were again a dwindled party. Cold and seasonable was the weather, with the ice bearing on the lake, the holly bright with berries, and now for the last time the Christmas hearth crackled for us with the glowing embers of the wood-fire, and our places at breakfast were piled with mutual presents, and after dinner the crackers were pulled. I can see my mother now, older than any in years, and the youngest of all in heart, shutting her eyes for the explosions as she tugged at the frilled end of her firework, and thereafter crowning herself with the pink paper cap that came out of one and blowing frantically on a small whistle from another. And, indeed, these feats were not to her only symbols and memorials of Christmases long ago, when she might be supposed to deck herself in these treasures in order to amuse her small children, by making herself bright with decoration and dizzy with blowing: she enjoyed it all immensely on her own account. This was Christmas, and all right-minded people behaved like that at this season. Already that morning she had been wakened by the servants singing carols outside her windows, and probably she would be kept awake that night by the sound of their revels as they played games in the hall and danced to the strains of an immense musical-box, as heavy as a loaded portmanteau, which played twelve different tunes. So there we all sat in our caps and tassels, and made a row with the toys, and when nobody could go on any longer, the whistles and the squeaking machines had to be collected by my mother to hang up in Joey's cage, so that he, too, like a Christian parrot, might take part in the jubilation. That was done, but Joey was not at all like a Christian parrot, for he cursed and swore at being disturbed, not rightly grasping the significance of these offerings. Then she and I played a peculiarly irritating form of patience, in which it was really hard to remember that you were a person of good breeding and self-control, and for a little while we sat round the fire, and looked forward to Arthur's being of the party again next year. It was past bedtime now, and the musical-box was merry.

As soon as I had seen my exposition of Turkish affairs through the press, I started gaily on those of Poland, and instantly descended into a bottomless pit of confusion. To pick your way about even, not to mention getting anywhere particular or escorting others there, was precisely like attempting in the dark to find a path through a wilderness of barbed wire. There were nineteen political parties in Poland, all at loggerheads with each other, and each clamouring for a different method of making a united Poland. If I got hold of what seemed an indisputable fact one day, it followed as a corollary that I should find a flat, indisputable contradiction of it the next, and it was not till I had wandered for weeks in the darkness, eternally impaling myself on barbed wire, that the faintest light began to dawn, and even that at first only more convincingly revealed to what an inextricable position I had come. The affairs of Turkey in comparison seemed like a broad and level high-road running straight and orderly between well-defined hedges: you only had to march on; here, for a road, were morasses and moving quick-sands.

Then by degrees some kind of mournful clearness brightened: I could get my chapters drafted, and I really thought I was coming to the end of trouble when M. Dmowski, the head of the National Democrats, who was then in London, most kindly read the whole manuscript and went through it with me, chapter by chapter. But then, when I took certain parts to a Polish expert at the Foreign Office for fuller elucidation, he, with a squirt of statistics, washed away the very foundation of the structure. He said that M. Dmowski's figures were all wrong, and M. Dmowski asserted that never had there been anything so incontrovertible as his figures. A very puzzling place was Poland. . . .

But during that spring there was always an escape for a day or two, and that to Tremans. There, somehow, the dusk and the madness of it all did not penetrate, not because my mother did not realize the darkness, but because a vaster light illumined her, that " clear shining after rain " which comes sometimes towards the end of life, which is death, towards death which is the beginning of life. She looked forward to no rounding by sleep, but to a far more vivid consciousness, and she writes in her diary of how coming back from an early celebration one Sunday morning, she would not have been surprised if she had met a delightful company of those who in their life had been in so close a communion with her. Out of her six children four already were waiting for her a little way ahead, and her husband was there, and more friends of her heart than now survived. There was no abatement in her love for those still with her, she still found the world fascinatingly interesting, she was well and very serenely happy.

It was in June when, after a considerable absence, I could get down home again. The Polish business, for good or bad, was finished, and the result, type-written, needed a week of correction and revision. So I wrote to my mother suggesting myself for a whole week, if she was sure that was convenient, and her answer was, " Oh, Fred: a whole week! Lovely! Come to your foolish but ever loving Ma." And, if it wouldn't be tiresome, would I read aloud in the evening what I had written about Poland? She wanted to hear it all: it was disgraceful not to know about Poland, and the *Times Atlas* must be fetched in order to arrive at complete comprehension, and might she take the last chapter up to bed with her, to be returned faithfully in the morning ? And the last evening came. " Oh, it has been a lovely week," she said. " Can't you come back very soon ? "

In the morning came the family ritual of departure, with wild wavings of hands as the car turned sharply round at the angle of the house, and I never imagined, I never guessed. . . . I went down for a week-end next day into Essex, after leaving Poland at the printer's, and in the slack after-breakfast hour on Sunday morning there came a telegram, summoning me back at once. Before I could start there came another.

She had died as she had always hoped she might. She had just got to bed on Saturday night, when God's hand was laid on her head. There was nothing left of her here but the small sweet raiment in which her spirit had dwelled. She had no more use for it, and had left it behind.

I thank God for her dear love, and her shining life, and her swift death.

www.ingramcontent.com/pod-product-compliance
Lightning Source LLC
Chambersburg PA
CBHW020830160426
43192CB00007B/594